Financial Analysis

The Next Step

Revised Edition

James O. Gill

Moira Chatton

A Fifty-Minute™ *Series Book*

CRISP.
Learning
Menlo Park, California

1-800-442-7477

CrispLearning.com

Financial Analysis

The Next Step

Revised Edition

James O. Gill
Moira Chatton

CREDITS:

Editor: **L.K. Woodbury**
Senior Editor: **Debbie Woodbury**
Copy Editor: **Charlotte Bosarge**
Production Manager: **Judy Petry**
Text Design: **Amy Shayne**
Cover: **Amy Shayne**
Cartoonist: **Ralph Mapson**
Production Artists: **Carol Lindahl, June Layton, Darin Stumme**

© 1992, 2001 Crisp Publications, Inc.
Printed in the United States of America by Von Hoffmann Graphics, Inc.

CrispLearning.com

01 02 03 04   10 9 8 7 6 5 4 3 2 1

Library of Congress Catalog Card Number 00-106653
Gill, James and Moira Chatton
Financial Analysis, Revised Edition
The Next Step
ISBN 1-56052-588-6

This book is printed on recyclable paper with soy ink.

Learning Objectives For:

Financial Analysis, Revised Edition

The objectives for *Financial Analysis, Revised Edition* are listed below. They have been developed to guide you, the reader, to the core issues covered in this book.

OBJECTIVES

❑ 1) Provide a quick review of the basics of financial analysis

❑ 2) Introduce you to the contents of corporate financial statements

❑ 3) Provide information about special statements such as inventory, depreciation, and retained earnings

❑ 4) Discuss ratios concerning capitalization by common stock

❑ 5) Show various ways that ratios interact when one is changed

❑ 6) Show how to use quick decision-making techniques

❑ 7) Provide tips on how to interpret an annual report

ASSESSING YOUR PROGRESS

In addition to the learning objectives, CrispLearning has developed an **assessment** that covers the fundamental information presented in this book. A twenty-five item, multiple choice/true-false questionnaire allows the reader to evaluate his or her comprehension of the subject matter. An answer sheet with a chart matching the questions to the listed objectives is also available. To learn how to obtain a copy of this assessment please call: **1-800-442-7477** and ask to speak with a Customer Service Representative.

Assessments should not be used in any selection process.

Preface

This book is a follow-up to *Understanding Financial Statements: A Primer of Useful Information.* It is written for someone who has a basic understanding of financial statements, knows the difference between cash and income, is familiar with the use of ratios, and can analyze expenses. These skills should be reviewed by either reading *Understanding Financial Statements,* taking a course in basic finance, or both.

The material and tools presented in this book should be reviewed several times. Go through the checklists and work the sample problems until you understand and feel comfortable with what is happening and why. Take it step-by-step; some of the concepts may be new, but with practice you will achieve a working relationship with each analytical tool. Your comprehension will help you know where and when to apply these tools and increase your understanding of the financial information available from corporations.

Good luck!

Moira Chatton

Moira E. Chatton

About the Authors

The late James O. Gill worked as Division Manager and Projects Manager with the Naval Weapons Support Center in Crane, Indiana. He was the author of *Financial Basics of Small Business Success, Financial Analysis*, and the first edition of *Understanding Financial Statements*, all published by Crisp Publications, Inc.

Moira E. Chatton has revised *Financial Analysis* as well as its companion book, *Understanding Financial Statements*. She earned a degree in biochemistry from the University of California, Berkeley, and an M.B.A. from the University of Georgia. Employed initially as a financial analyst by Chevron Chemical Company in San Francisco, she held a series of increasingly responsible and challenging positions in other Chevron companies. Since retiring from Chevron, Ms. Chatton provides in-house financial training to local businesses and teaches small business and finance courses at Santa Rosa Junior College and the University of Phoenix.

Introduction

Business is constantly facing new challenges; never with greater frequency than today. International competition, technology that didn't even exist a few years ago, regulations from environmental and safety agencies, and globalization make it difficult to stay in business, let alone *grow* a business. You can't stop taking risks, but you can minimize them by giving more attention to the financial implications of each decision.

That's what this book is about. It is designed to provide easy-to-follow instructions to analyze your financial position and make it better. It can also be used as a reference manual. It provides definitions and explains terms that you, as an aspiring manager or small business owner, may hear during meetings or business conversations. It provides examples to increase your understanding, and it will help you speak with confidence about the affairs of your company.

As you use the tools in this book, you will discover which ones can be most beneficial to you. Please, do not try to memorize all of them. There is no exam or final grade. These tools are to be applied to the actual situations you encounter on your job. A calculator will be helpful when you work through the examples and the review at the end of each part of this book.

Financial Analysis: The Next Step is designed to teach a new or experienced manager how to be a better manager by providing the tools to analyze your part of the business, make better decisions, and help you understand the terms and language of financial statements and analysis. Your efforts to understand and use these tools will help make you more effective on the job and an important member of the management team!

Contents

Part 1: Reviewing The Basics
A Quick Refresher 3
The Balance Sheet Equation 4
Glossary of Balance Sheet Terms 5
The Income Statement 7
Glossary of Income Statement Terms 8
Ratios and Percentages 9
Review 15

Part 2: Corporate Financial Statements
The Consolidated Statement 21
Your Company's Consolidated Statement 23
Analysis 24
Glossary of Additional Terms 26
The Income Statement 27
Your Company's Income Statement 28
Changes in Financial Position 29
Your Company's Changes in Balance Sheet Accounts 30
Analysis 31
The Cash Flow Statement 32
Your Company's Cash Flow Statement 34
The Statement of Retained Earnings 35
Checklist 36

Part 3: Asset Management
Management of Current Assets 39
Managing Receivables Policy 40
JOG Corporation Notes 42
Projected Analysis for Your Company 44
Calculations 45
Inventory Valuation Methods 46
Valuing Your Company's Inventory 49
Depreciation 50
Review 53

Part 4: New Ratios
Ratios Help Make Decisions 57
Capital Stock/Market Ratios 58
Limitations of Ratio Use 66
Review 67

Part 5: The Interaction of Ratios
How Ratios Affect Each Other 71
The Makeup of Ratios 76
Checklist 77

Part 6: Financial Planning
Financial Planning 81
Break-Even Analysis 82
Margin of Safety 86
Leverage 87
Financial Leverage 89
Drawbacks to Using Break-Even Analysis 91
Decision-Tree Analysis 92
Example of Decision-Tree Analysis 93
Cost-Benefit Analysis 97
Review 99

Part 7: Reading an Annual Report
How to Read an Annual Report 103
Checklist 108

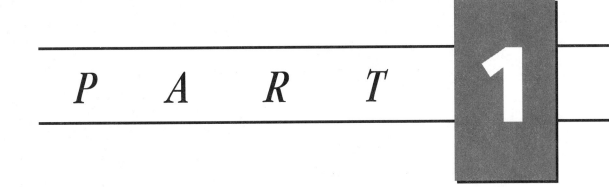

P A R T 1

Reviewing
the Basics

A Quick Refresher

This part of the book is a quick review of the basics covered in the previous book, *Understanding Financial Statements*. This review will help you make the transition to a more complex balance sheet (sometimes called a statement of financial position) and income statement (often called a profit and loss statement or P&L).

In most corporate income statements, accounts are consolidated. This means that all revenues no matter what division or subsidiary they apply to are added together to reflect the parent company's total revenues. The same holds true for expenses. Detailed financial information, useful to individual managers, isn't always presented in an annual report, but managers usually receive an "internal" report detailing financial data relative to his or her area. If you get these reports at work and wish to analyze them, you can use the analysis techniques covered in the basic book, *Understanding Financial Statements*. That book is available from Crisp Publications, Inc., 1200 Hamilton Court, Menlo Park, California 94025, or from your bookstore.

If you are familiar with basic ratio and expense analysis, Part 1 of this book will serve as a quick refresher for you. Depending on your level of expertise, you may want to move directly on to Part 2, on page 21.

The Balance Sheet Equation

The basic formula is:

> Assets = Liabilities + Shareholders' Equity (often called Net Worth)

A simple balance sheet looks like this:

XYZ HARDWARE AND BUILDING SUPPLY BALANCE SHEET YEAR END 20XX				
ASSETS			**LIABILITIES**	
Current Assets			*Current Liabilities*	
Cash	$ 2,000		Notes Payable	$ 18,000
Accounts Receivable	85,000		Accts Payable	205,000
Inventory	210,000		Accruals	6,000
Total Current Assets	$ 297,000		Total Current Liabilities	$ 229,000
Fixed Assets			*Long-Term Debt*	
Land/Bldg	$ 60,000		Mortgage	$ 25,000
Equip/Fix	55,000		Total Long-Term Debt	$ 25,000
Depreciation	(15,000)			
Total Fixed Assets	$ 100,000			
			Shareholders' Equity	$ 143,000
Total Assets	**$ 397,000**		**Total Liab & Equity**	**$ 397,000**

The balance sheet shows *assets, liabilities,* and *shareholders'* or *owners' equity.* The assets are divided into *current assets* and *fixed* or *long-term assets.* The liabilities are divided into *current liabilities* and *long-term debt.* The shareholders' equity is the difference between assets and liabilities.

Note: Assets = Liabilities + Shareholders' Equity. Assets are what a company owns. *Liabilities* and *Shareholders' Equity* tells you how the company has paid for what it owns. Liabilities represent debt to outsiders, such as banks and other lenders. *Shareholders' Equity* represents what owners have invested in the company.

Glossary of Balance Sheet Terms

Accounts payable
Sometimes called trade payables, these are the total of all monies owed by the company to suppliers or vendors for raw material, products, services, or merchandise.

Accounts receivable
The monies owed to the company (but not yet collected) for merchandise or products sold, or services performed.

Accruals
Expenses, such as taxes or wages, that are accumulated against current profits but not yet due to be paid.

Assets
The money, merchandise, receipts, land, buildings, and equipment that a company owns and that have monetary value. Assets are represented on the balance sheet at their historic cost (what the company paid for them).

Cash
Money a business has control of and access to.

Current assets
The sum of cash, notes, and accounts receivable (minus reserves for bad debts), advances on inventories, inventories, and any other item that can be converted into cash in a short time, usually less than a year.

Current liabilities
The total of all monies owed by the company that will fall due within one year.

Depreciation
The estimated decrease in value of a fixed asset over its useful life. This is classified as an expense on the income statement, thus reducing taxes. You will learn more about this in Part 3.

Fixed assets
Land, buildings, building equipment, fixtures, machinery, tools, furniture, office devices, patterns, drawings; minus depreciation.

Inventory
For a manufacturing firm, it is the sum of finished merchandise on hand, raw material, and material in process. For retailers and wholesalers, it is the stock of goods on hand that are for sale.

Glossary of Balance Sheet Terms (CONTINUED)

Liabilities
Liabilities are the company's debts. They include notes payable, accounts payable, and accruals. There are two categories of liabilities: current liabilities and long-term debt.

Long-term debt
Sometimes called long-term liabilities, this represents all the obligations such as mortgages, bonds, term loans, and any other monies that come due more than one year from the date of the balance sheet.

Mortgage
A legal document that pledges property (as security or collateral) to cover a debt.

Notes payable
Money borrowed by the company that is to be paid back within one year.

Salvage value
The estimated price for which a fixed asset can be sold at the end of its useful life.

Shareholders' Equity or Owners' Equity
What the owners (the shareholders) have left when all the company's liabilities have been met. It is represented on a balance sheet as the difference between total assets and total liabilities. *Also called Net Worth, but remember this does not represent market or appraised value as most assets and liabilities appear on the balance sheet at their historic cost.*

The Income Statement

Shown below is a simple profit and loss statement for a sole proprietorship:

PROFIT AND LOSS STATEMENT YEAR END 20XX		
Net Sales (Minus Allowances and Discounts)		$ 700,000
Cost of Goods Sold		500,000
Gross Profit		200,000
Expenses		
Drawings (Owner's salary)	$ 74,000	
Wages	65,000	
Delivery	7,000	
Bad Debt	4,000	
Telephone	2,000	
Depreciation	4,000	
Insurance	7,000	
Taxes (Local)	8,000	
Interest	8,700	
Advertising	3,000	
Miscellaneous	2,000	
Total Expenses	$ 184,700	
Net Earnings (Before Federal Taxes)		**$ 15,300**

The corporate statement looks like this:

JOG CORPORATION – INCOME STATEMENT YEAR END 20XX	
Net Sales	$21,108,000
Cost of Goods Sold	13,546,000
Gross Profit	7,562,000
Operating expenses	4,958,000
Operating Profit	2,604,000
Interest charges	278,000
Earnings before taxes	2,326,000
Income taxes (35%)	814,100
Net earnings	1,511,900
Retained earnings at the beginning of the year	3,080,000
	4,591,900
Dividends paid	300,000
($.30/share; 1,000,000 shares outstanding)	
Retained earnings at the end of the year	**$ 4,291,900**

Glossary of Income Statement Terms

Cost of goods sold
For a retail or wholesale business, it is the total price paid for the products sold during the accounting period, plus the cost of having the products delivered to the store. For a manufacturing firm, it is the beginning inventory plus purchases, delivery costs, material, labor, and overhead, minus the ending inventory.

Dividend
The portion of a corporation's net earnings paid to shareholders at a specified rate per share.

Earnings before interest and taxes (EBIT)
As used in this book, it refers to earnings before interest costs or federal taxes are deducted.

Earnings before taxes (or Net profit)
As used in this book, it refers to the profit before paying federal taxes.

Expenses
The cost of doing business. It includes such items as wages, telephone, insurance, depreciation, interest, and advertising. Often called *operating expenses.*

Gross profit
The profit before expenses, interest, other charges, and federal taxes have been deducted.

Net earnings
The amount left over after deducting all due bills for the accounting period and paying off all due interest and federal taxes.

Net sales
The total dollar value of all sales minus returns, allowances, discounts, and rebates. *Net sales rather than gross sales are used to reflect the actual economic or revenue generating sales of the company.*

Retained earnings
The portion of a corporation's net earnings not paid to shareholders in the form of dividends. Retained earnings are reinvested in the company. They accumulate over the life of the company.

Ratios and Percentages

Ratios compare one thing to another. They establish a relationship or correlation. For instance, if you want to know what percent of sales the net earnings are, simply divide the amount of sales dollars (the base figure, bottom number, or denominator) into the amount of net earnings (top number or numerator). For example, if the sales are $700,000 and the net earnings is $15,300, the percentage is:

$$\frac{\$15,300}{\$700,000} \quad = \quad \frac{2.2}{100} \quad = \quad 2.2\%$$

The base number need not be the larger number. For example, the ratio of sales to assets: if the sales are $700,000 and the assets are $397,000, the assets generated sales of 1.8 times the assets' value, there is a "turnover" of 1.8 times.

$$\frac{\$700,000}{\$397,000} \quad = \quad 1.8 \text{ times}$$

Note: If the top number is smaller than the bottom number, the ratio will be less than 1 and expressed as a percentage. If the top number is larger than the bottom number, the ratio will be greater than 1 and expressed as "times."

In this book the following ratios will be discussed:

➤ Liquidity Ratios

➤ Profitability Ratios

➤ Efficiency Ratios

Liquidity Ratios

Liquidity ratios measure the amount of cash or investments that can be converted to cash in order to pay expenses, bills, and other obligations as they come due.

The *current ratio* measures the ability of the company to meet short-term obligations which means to pay off its short-term debt. *Remember, current means in less than one year.*

$$\text{Current ratio} \quad = \quad \frac{\text{Current assets}}{\text{Current liabilities}}$$

A low current ratio may indicate a lack of cash to pay off debt and to take advantage of discounts.

A high current ratio does not necessarily mean a company is in good shape. It could mean that its cash is not being productive. Also, it does not indicate the quality of receivables or inventory which may account for the high ratio.

A quick version of the current ratio eliminates inventory, and sometimes accounts receivable, from the current assets. This gives a conservative number. This ratio is more appropriate than the current ratio for a company with excess or obsolete inventory. It is also better to use for companies with questionable receivables.

Try both before deciding which version to use, and look closely at the status of accounts receivable and inventory.

The *turnover of cash ratio* measures the adequacy of the company's working capital, which is required to pay bills and to finance sales. The working capital is the current assets minus the current liabilities.

$$\text{Turnover of cash ratio} \quad = \quad \frac{\text{Net sales}}{\text{Working capital}}$$

A low turnover of cash ratio means that the company has funds tied up in short-term, low-yielding assets, and can get by with less cash.

A high ratio could mean an inability to pay company bills.

The *debt to equity ratio* measures total debt coverage. It expresses the relationship between the capital contributed by the creditors and that contributed by the shareholders.

$$\text{Debt to equity ratio} \quad = \quad \frac{\text{Total debt}}{\text{Shareholders' Equity}}$$

Remember, **total debt** *is the same as total liabilities;* **shareholders' equity** *is total assets less total liabilities.*

A low debt to equity ratio would indicate that the company could borrow money more easily. It could also mean that the company is too conservative.

A high ratio indicates that most of the risk in the business is assumed by the creditors. Obtaining money from outside sources, such as a bank, will be more difficult.

Profitability Ratios

Profitability ratios measure and help control income.

The *net profit ratio* measures the effectiveness of management. Filtering out the effects of debt and taxes is useful for two reasons. One, taxes may be higher or lower because of events other than the operation of the business. Two, high debt payments, such as those found in a new or start-up business, could distort earnings, so that a comparison to another company is skewed.

$$\text{Net profit ratio} \quad = \quad \frac{\text{Earnings before interest and taxes (EBIT)}}{\text{Net sales}}$$

A low net profit ratio is not good. It could indicate that expenses are too high to be covered by the sales volume. The age of a business is important when evaluating this ratio. As you have seen with many new Internet companies, profits may not exist today, but the public expects earnings to increase in the future.

A high ratio indicates either that expenses are being held down or that the company may be getting more out of its assets and debt.

The *rate of return on sales* measures how much net profit was derived from each sales dollar. It can provide an idea of the coverage of fixed costs. It can also indicate whether expenses are being held down. It is very important to consider the industry when evaluating this ratio. For example, grocery stores have a considerably lower rate of return on sales than aircraft manufacturers.

$$\text{Rate of return on sales} = \frac{\text{Net earnings before taxes (EBIT)}}{\text{Net sales}}$$

A low rate of return on sales is not necessarily bad if your industry operates on low margins and high volume.

A high rate is usually good if other things are in line—if payments on debt are kept up, assets are well-maintained and replaced as needed, and other expenses are not deferred.

The *rate of return on investment* measures how much net earnings before taxes was derived from the shareholders' investment in the company.

$$\text{Rate of return on investment} = \frac{\text{Net earnings before taxes}}{\text{Shareholders' equity}}$$

A low rate of return on investment means that another investment may be better. It could indicate that management is inefficient or that the company is too conservative and not earning up to its potential.

A high rate indicates that borrowing may be the source of much of the capitalization, that management is extremely efficient, or that the firm is undercapitalized.

The *rate of return on assets* measures the net earnings before taxes that is generated by the assets of the business.

$$\text{Rate of return on assets} = \frac{\text{Net earnings before taxes}}{\text{Total assets}}$$

A low rate of return on assets indicates poor performance or poor use of the assets by management.

A high rate indicates good performance and good use of assets.

Watch out if the fixed assets of the business are heavily depreciated. This could mean that the assets are old. Also, beware if there is a large amount of unusual expenses or income. This could indicate that the current performance is not typical, but based on an unusual occurrence.

Efficiency Ratios

Efficiency ratios measure how well the business is being conducted. They provide quick indications of how well the company's credit policy is working and its inventory is moving. They help keep the business in balance.

The following ratio measures the time it takes to collect outstanding receivables:

$$\frac{\text{Accounts receivable} \times 365 \text{ days per year}}{\text{Net sales}}$$

A high ratio shows that it takes too many days to collect the company's money. This means that working capital/cash will be low and some bills may not get paid.

A low ratio means that the credit sales are being collected fast and that more money is in the company and working to the shareholders' advantage.

The *inventory turnover rate* measures how fast the merchandise is moving.

$$\text{Inventory turnover rate} \ = \ \frac{\text{Cost of goods sold}}{\text{Average inventory}} \quad or \quad \frac{\text{Net sales}}{\text{Average inventory}}$$

A low rate of inventory turnover indicates that too much money may be tied up in goods and storage and not working as hard as it could.

A high rate indicates that sales are booming—or that sales are lost because merchandise was not available.

The *fixed assets to equity ratio* measures the portion of shareholders' equity that is made up of fixed (long-term) assets. It provides an indication of how much capital is tied up in buildings, fixtures, equipment, etc.

$$\text{Fixed assets to equity ratio} \ = \ \frac{\text{Fixed assets}}{\text{Shareholders' equity}}$$

A low fixed assets to equity ratio indicates that the shareholders' equity may be more liquid and easier to obtain in the event of bankruptcy or tight financial times.

A high ratio indicates that the shareholders' part of the company may be brick and mortar or a piece of equipment. The company may be in need of additional working capital.

The *investment turnover ratio* measures the amount of sales generated by the assets. This ratio is very dependent on the industry being evaluated. Businesses which require heavy investment in capital equipment such as oil refineries will have a much lower ratio than industries that are less capital intensive, such as software firms.

$$\text{Investment turnover ratio} = \frac{\text{Net sales}}{\text{Total assets}}$$

A low investment turnover ratio may indicate that there are too many assets and too few sales.

A high ratio may mean that something good is happening. The company is experiencing more sales without investing in more equipment or buildings, or obtaining more cash.

Capital stock/market ratios will be discussed in Part 4.

Limitations on the Use of Ratio Analysis

The preceding pages have given you a review of some of the more frequently used financial ratios. They help us understand a company's financial position. Financial ratios are useful tools when evaluating a business. But, we must be aware of some important limitations involved with their use. These limitations are discussed at the end of Part 4 of this book. Please review them before making judgments about a particular company's financial condition based on its financial ratios.

Review

Do you remember? Write your answers in the spaces provided.

1. The balance sheet equation?

   _____

   _____

2. The two types of assets?

   _____

   _____

3. The two types of liabilities?

   _____

   _____

4. The definition of accounts receivable?

   _____

   _____

5. The definition of inventory?

   _____

   _____

6. The definition of long-term debt?

   _____

   _____

7. The definition of cost of goods sold?

   _____

   _____

8. The definition of gross profit?

   _____

   _____

9. The definition of net earnings?

   _____

   _____

10. The two ways that ratios are expressed?

    _____

    _____

The answers are on page 17.

PRACTICE PROBLEMS

Before moving on, you may want to brush up on working and interpreting some ratios. Based on the following figures, calculate the ratios indicated below. Give a brief analysis of each ratio you calculate.

Current assets	$ 524,000	Net earnings before taxes	$ 18,000
Current liabilities	302,000	Total assets	1,129,000
Net sales	1,545,000	Accounts receivable	278,000
	Working capital (current assets-current liabilities)		222,000

Example: Current ratio:

$$\frac{\text{Current assets}}{\text{Current liabilities}} = \frac{\$524,000}{\$302,000} = 1.7 \text{ times}$$

Analysis: _____

1. Turnover of cash ratio:

$$\frac{\text{Net sales}}{\text{Working capital}} \quad = \qquad\qquad = \qquad \text{times}$$

Analysis: _____

2. Rate of return on sales:

$$\frac{\text{Net earnings before taxes}}{\text{Net sales}} \quad = \qquad\qquad = \qquad \%$$

Analysis: _____

3. Rate of return on assets:

$$\frac{\text{Net earnings before taxes}}{\text{Total assets}} \quad = \qquad\qquad = \qquad \%$$

Analysis: _____

4. Time to collect outstanding receivables:

$$\frac{\text{Accounts receivable x 365}}{\text{Net sales}} \quad = \qquad\qquad = \qquad \text{days}$$

Analysis: _____

5. Investment turnover ratio:

$$\frac{\text{Net sales}}{\text{Total assets}} \quad = \qquad\qquad = \qquad \text{times}$$

Analysis: _____

The answers are on page 18.

Answers to Review

1. Assets = Liabilities + Shareholders' equity.

2. Current assets and fixed assets.

3. Current liabilities and long-term debt.

4. Accounts receivable are the monies owed to the company (but not yet collected) for merchandise, products, or services sold or performed.

5. Inventory for a manufacturing firm is the sum of finished merchandise on hand, raw material, and material in process. For retailers and wholesalers, it is the stock of goods on hand that are for sale.

6. Long-term debt is all the obligations such as mortgages, bonds, term loans, and any other monies that come due more than one year from the date of the balance sheet.

7. Cost of goods sold, for a retail or wholesale business, is the total price paid for the products sold during the accounting period, plus the cost of having the products delivered to the store. For a manufacturing firm it is the beginning inventory plus purchases, delivery costs, material, labor, and overhead, minus the ending inventory.

8. Gross profit is the profit before expenses, interest, other charges, and federal taxes have been deducted.

9. Net earnings is the amount left over after paying off all due bills for the accounting period, and paying off all due interest and federal taxes.

10. If the top number is smaller than the bottom number, the ratio will be a percentage. If the top number is larger than the bottom number, the ratio will be expressed as "times."

ANSWERS TO PRACTICE PROBLEMS

1. $$\frac{\text{Net sales}}{\text{Working capital}} = \frac{\$1,545,000}{\$222,000} = 7.0 \text{ times}$$

    Analysis: **The working capital appears adequate to support the sales volume.**

2. $$\frac{\text{Net earnings before taxes}}{\text{Net sales}} = \frac{\$18,000}{\$1,545,000} = 1.2 \%$$

    Analysis: **This is a low profit. Further analysis is warranted to determine why.**

3. $$\frac{\text{Net earnings before taxes}}{\text{Total assets}} = \frac{\$18,000}{\$1,129,000} = 1.6 \%$$

    Analysis: **The company is not getting a good return on its assets.**

4. $$\frac{\text{Accounts receivable x 365}}{\text{Net sales}} = \frac{\$278,000 \text{ x } 365}{\$1,545,000} = 66 \text{ days}$$

    Analysis: **The company should tighten up and start collecting these outstanding accounts. With more cash, current liabilities may be paid faster and this will improve the current ratio.**

5. $$\frac{\text{Net sales}}{\text{Total assets}} = \frac{\$1,545,000}{\$1,129,000} = 1.4 \text{ times}$$

    Analysis: **Too many assets chasing too few sales. The return on assets should be several times higher.**

P A R T 2

Corporate

Financial

Statements

The Consolidated Statement

A corporate balance sheet is usually consolidated. This means that it has only the major accounts listed on the balance sheet, such as cash, securities, accounts receivable, property/equipment, and maybe other assets listed on the asset side; and current liabilities, long-term debt, and shareholders' equity on the liabilities side. The accounts of every division, or other companies owned by the parent corporation, are added together and included in the consolidated accounts and not separately identified.

Let's take a look at a balance sheet for JOG Corporation.

JOG CORPORATION CONSOLIDATED STATEMENT YEAR END 20XX					
	Yr 2	**Yr 1**		**Yr 2**	**Yr 1**
Current Assets	$(000)		**Current Liabilities**	$(000)	
Cash	1,270	773	Notes payable	500	400
Gov't securities	407	100	Accts payable	408	873
Accts receivable	3,233	2,700	Accrued expenses	449	650
Inventories			Accrued taxes	500	999
Finished merch	3,300	4,030	Total current liabilities	1,857	2,922
Work in process	775	944			
Raw mtl/supplies	315	564	Long-term Debt		
Goods in transit	175	238	15-year notes	1,150	1,050
	4,565	5,776	10-year notes	1,000	900
Total current assets	9,475	9,349	Total long-term debt	2,150	1,950
Property and Equipment					
Land	482	549	**Shareholders' Equity**		
Buildings	418	418	Capital stock $1 par		
Equipment	1,157	1,267	value (2,500,000 auth)		
	2,057	2,234	1,013,000 outstanding		
Depreciation	903	985	Yr 1; 1,033,000 Yr 2	1,033	1,013
Total fixed assets	1,154	1,249	Paid-in capital	2,167	1,987
Other Assets			Retained earnings	4,092	3,080
Prepaid expenses	114	104	Total shareholders'		
Foreign receipts	556	250	equity	7,292	6,080
Total other assets	670	354			
			Total liabilities		
Total assets	**11,299**	**10,952**	**and equity**	**11,299**	**10,952**

The Consolidated Statement (CONTINUED)

The balance sheet describes the financial condition of a company as of a particular date. The assets, or those things the company owns and has the right to use, are listed on the left side or the top of the balance sheet, usually in descending order of liquidity. That is, cash is first and fixed assets and intangibles are listed last. Intangibles consist of trademarks, patents, goodwill, options to buy property, etc. Goodwill is only created when one company purchases another for an amount that is greater than the value of the net assets. For example, when one company buys another, they usually pay more than the value of the purchased company's assets. This can result from the good name, or reputation of the purchased company, creating value to the buyer.

On the right side of or below the assets on the balance sheet are liabilities and shareholders' equity. Those liabilities that must be paid first appear at the top. Current liabilities are listed before long-term debt. Since the shareholders must wait to see if there is any money left before receiving their dividends, the shareholders' equity is at the bottom.

Begin your analysis of the balance sheet by examining the major categories listed above. For instance, JOG Corporation's current assets increased slightly from year 1 to year 2. Fixed assets (property and equipment) and other assets declined slightly. This in itself appears not too significant. However, cash increased and inventories declined by good-sized margins. This puts the corporation in a very liquid position. In fact, some more money should go to lowering debt, increasing sales, and upgrading equipment and facilities—or paying higher dividends. Generally this balance sheet shows the company to be conservative and profitable.

Your Company's Consolidated Statement

Place your company's information here. If you want to use different titles than those listed below, simply add those you feel appropriate.

_____ (COMPANY NAME)
CONSOLIDATED STATEMENT
YEAR END 20___

	Yr 2	Yr 1		Yr 2	Yr 1
Current Assets	$(000)		**Current Liabilities**	$(000)	
Cash			Notes payable		
Gov't securities			Accts payable		
Accts receivable			Accrued expenses		
Inventories			Accrued taxes		
Other	_____	_____	Other	_____	_____
Total current assets			Total current liabilities		
Property and Equipment			**Long-term debt**	_____	_____
Land					
Buildings			Total long-term debt		
Equipment	_____	_____			
Depreciation	_____	_____	**Shareholders' Equity**		
Total fixed assets			Capital stock		
Other Assets			Paid-in capital		
Prepaid expenses			Retained earnings	_____	_____
Other	_____	_____	Total shareholders' equity		
Total other assets					
Total assets	=====	=====	**Total liabilities and equity**	=====	=====

Analysis

Another way of looking at major categories is to break them down into percentages, like this:

JOG CORPORATION YEAR 2			
Current assets	84%	Current liabilities	16%
Fixed assets	10%	Long-term debt	19%
Other assets	6%	Shareholders' equity	65%
Total assets	100%	Total liabilities and equity	100%

Traditionally, a *safe corporation* has a low return, a large equity base and slow growth, with little debt and short-term assets.

A SAFE CORPORATION			
Current assets	70%	Current liabilities	25%
Fixed assets	30%	Long-term debt	15%
		Shareholders' equity	60%

A *risk corporation* generally has a high yield, high long-term assets, outside funds supporting over one-half of the business, a small equity base, fast growth, and large earnings fluctuations.

A RISK CORPORATION			
Current assets	30%	Current liabilities	20%
Fixed assets	70%	Long-term debt	45%
		Shareholders' equity	35%

Note: These ratios may vary considerably depending on the industry.

Is your company a safe company or is it a risk company? Use the figures from the balance sheet to calculate the percentages.

Current assets _____ %   Current liabilities _____ %

Fixed assets _____ %   Long-term debt _____ %

Other assets _____ %   Shareholders' equity _____ %

How would you characterize your corporation, based on these figures?

_____

_____

_____

_____

_____

Look through some corporate annual reports you may have around the house or at work. Use the calculations outlined above to determine if the companies are "safe" or "risk" corporations. Are your results consistent with your impressions of the corporations?

Glossary of Additional Terms

Additional paid-in capital
When it's first issued, a share of stock usually sells above its par value. The amount in excess of the par value is known as additional paid-in capital.

Capital stock
The total amount invested in the business in exchange for shares of stock up to par value.

Common stock
Usually means ownership in the company. The more shares of common stock a shareholder has, the greater is that shareholder's voting power. There is no promise of dividend payments or return of the investor's investment.

Foreign receipts
Money that comes in from a company's foreign subsidiaries.

Other assets
On the example balance sheet, other assets are those tangible items that are not a part of any other category.

Par value
The face value of a stock at the time it was issued. Subsequent selling prices are usually different from the par value. A stock does not have to have a par value designation.

Preferred stock
Usually, dividends are paid to holders of preferred stock before they are paid to holders of common stock. Also, if the company declares bankruptcy, holders of preferred stock have a claim on the assets of the business before the common stock holders.

Prepaid expenses
Those expenses that carry into the next accounting period. They may be rents, insurance, subscriptions, wages, etc.

Shareholders' equity
The total dollar amount of the company's outstanding common stock and preferred stock, additional paid-in capital, and retained earnings as listed on the company's balance sheet. (JOG Corporation has no preferred stock.)

Note: These definitions should be checked with your company's accounting personnel to make sure they match the company's usage. If not, use your company's terminology. For example, some companies use the term *capital surplus* instead of *additional paid-in capital*.

The Income Statement

The income statement, often called the *profit and loss statement* or *P&L,* reports on the company's profitability for a period of time, generally a year. Net sales are listed first followed by expenses. For manufacturing companies, the first expense is the cost of goods sold. Some companies provide a separate statement accompanying the income statement for cost of goods sold alone, as it can be rather complex. For most other companies it is fairly simple: purchases minus returns, discounts, and rebates, plus freight-in. This figure is added to the beginning inventory. The next step is to subtract the ending inventory. The remainder is cost of goods sold.

Here is an income statement for JOG Corporation:

JOG CORPORATION INCOME STATEMENT YEAR END 20XX		
	Yr 2	Yr 1
1. Net sales	$21,108,000	$15,033,000
2. Cost of goods sold	13,546,000	9,692,000
3. Gross profit (1 – 2)	7,562,000	5,341,000
4. Operating expenses	4,958,000	3,754,000
5. Earnings before interest and taxes (EBIT) (3 – 4)	2,604,000	1,587,000
6. Interest charges	278,000	53,000
7. Earnings before taxes (5 – 6)	2,326,000	1,534,000
8. Income taxes (35%)	814,000	537,000
9. Net earnings (7 – 8)	1,512,000	997,000
10. Retained earnings at the beginning of the year	3,080,000	2,392,000
11. Total (9 + 10)	4,592,000	3,389,000
12. Dividends paid	500,000	309,000
13. Retained earnings at the end of the year (11 – 12)	$ 4,092,000	$ 3,080,000

In year 2, JOG Corporation's net earnings were 7.2% of net sales. The cost of goods sold was 64% of net sales. The gross profit was 36% of net sales. The earnings before taxes were 11% of net sales. The company paid dividends of 2.4% of net sales. These percentages are useful when analyzing your company's performance annually (trend analysis) or when comparing your company with other companies in the same industry.

Your Company's Income Statement

Create your company's income statement here.

_____ (COMPANY NAME)		
CONSOLIDATED STATEMENT		
YEAR END 20___		

	Yr 2	Yr 1
Net sales	_____	_____
Cost of goods sold	_____	_____
Gross profit		
Operating expenses		
Depreciation	_____	_____
Earnings before interest and tax (EBIT)		
Interest charges	_____	_____
Earnings before taxes		
Income taxes	_____	_____
Net earnings		
Retained earnings at the beginning of the year	_____	_____
Total		
Dividends paid	_____	_____
Retained earnings at the end of the year		

Changes in Financial Position

Now we'll look at how JOG Corporation's financial position changed between year 1 and year 2. We'll begin by analyzing changes in the balance sheet accounts. Cash flows into a company by increases in liabilities, like borrowing money; or by decreases in assets, such as accounts receivable. Cash flows out when there is a decrease in a liability, such as paying off some debt; or an increase in an asset, such as adding more accounts receivable or inventory or buying more equipment.

Balance Sheet Item	Yr 1 Begin	Yr 2 End	Cash Effect In	Cash Effect Out
CHANGES IN BALANCE SHEET ACCOUNTS				
Asset Accounts from the Balance Sheet			$(000's)	
Cash	773	1,270		497
Gov't securities	100	407		307
Accounts receivable	2,700	3,233		533
Finished material	4,030	3,300	730	
Work in process	944	775	169	
Raw material/supplies	564	315	249	
Goods in transit	238	175	63	
Land	549	482	67	
Buildings	418	418		
Equipment	1,267	1,157	110	
Depreciation	985	903		82
Prepaid expenses	104	114		10
Foreign receipts	250	556		306
Liabilities and Shareholders' Equity from the Balance Sheet				
Notes payable	400	500	100	
Accts payable	873	408		465
Accrued expenses	650	449		201
Accrued taxes	999	500		499
15-year notes	1,050	1,150	100	
10-year notes	900	1,000	100	
Shareholders' Equity				
Common stock outstanding	1,013	1,033	20	
Paid-in capital	1,987	2,167	180	
Retained earnings	3,080	4,092	1,012	
Total Changes in Balance Sheet Accounts			**2,900**	**2,900**

Your Company's Changes in Balance Sheet Accounts

Write in your company's changes in balance sheet accounts here.

Remember: Cash flows in when there is an *increase in liabilities* or a *decrease in assets*. Cash flows out when there is a *decrease in liabilities* or an *increase in assets*.

	Yr 1	Yr 2	Cash Effect	
Balance Sheet Item	**Begin**	**End**	**In**	**Out**
Asset Accounts from the Balance Sheet		$(000's)		
Cash				
Gov't securities				
Accounts receivable				
Finished material				
Work in process				
Raw material/supplies				
Goods in transit				
Land				
Buildings				
Equipment				
Depreciation				
Prepaid expenses				
Foreign receipts				
Liabilities and Shareholders' Equity from the Balance Sheet				
Notes payable				
Accts payable				
Accrued expenses				
Accrued taxes				
15-year notes				
10-year notes				
Shareholders' Equity				
Common stock outstanding				
Paid-in capital				
Retained earnings				
Total Changes in Balance Sheet Accounts				

CHANGES IN BALANCE SHEET ACCOUNTS

Analysis

From our calculations as shown on JOG's changes in balance sheet accounts, we see that JOG Corporation increased liquidity by increasing cash and decreasing inventory. This, along with reducing current liabilities, will help the quick ratio. The corporation aligned their fixed assets somewhat, with a small sell-off of land and equipment. The company increased long-term debt a little, reduced inventory, and increased income. JOG Corporation gained an increase in cash and marketable securities of almost $800,000.

Changes in balance sheet accounts provide an indication of the year-end actions taken and how they were paid. A drawback is that several short-term loans may have been taken out and paid off during the year, but they can't be seen separately. Also, these changes give no indication of whether the increased profits were due to volume or price increase, reduced cost of goods sold, or whether expenses were held down. These and other questions need to be answered by ratio and expense analyses.

The Cash Flow Statement

Much of the data we have calculated can be used to develop the cash flow statement. This statement divides a company's cash flows for an accounting period into three activities: operating, investing, and financing.

Operating activities are all cash flows related to the day-to-day operations of a business. They include collections from customers, payments to suppliers for the procuring of materials and supplies, and other operating cash flows such as advertising, administrative costs, interest, and tax payments. Interest received would also be included here.

Investing activities are cash flows used to purchase property and equipment for the company. It is the cash that a company uses to invest in itself to grow the business. On the other hand, cash generated from the sale of assets is considered cash in from investing.

Financing activities reflects cash flows, either in or out, from the company's investors, both lenders of debt and owners.

The cash flow statement deals with cash and marketable securities. It shows relationships among the cash flows from operating, investing, and financial activities. It delves into the question of whether the firm is generating cash to meet current and future needs. As a result, it has become one of the most important sources of information available from companies today.

Depreciation is an important element of this statement. Depreciation is deducted from income for tax purposes, but is added back to net income as a noncash item to obtain an estimate of the cash flow from operations.

Let's look at a cash flow statement for JOG Corporation:

JOG CORPORATION CASH FLOW STATEMENT YEAR END 20XX	
Operations	**$(000's)**
Net profit	1,512
Add: Depreciation expense	82
Decrease in inventories	1,211
Increase in notes payable*	100
Increase in long-term debt*	200
Minus: Increase in accounts receivable	(533)
Increase in prepaid expenses	(10)
Increased foreign receipts	(306)
Decrease in accounts payable	(465)
Decrease in accrued expenses	(201)
Decrease in accrued taxes	(499)
Total cash from operations	1,091
Investing	
Decrease in fixed assets**	95
Increased outlay for equipment	(82)
Total cash from investing	13
Financing	
Increased common stock	20
Increased paid-in capital	180
Paid dividends	(500)
Total cash from financing	(300)
Increase in cash and marketable securities	$ 804

*Sometimes put under financing activities

**Sometimes put under operating activities

Note: The decrease in fixed assets due to depreciation is calculated: Land $67,000 + equipment $110,000 − depreciation $82,000 = $95,000. The depreciation charge is also shown as increased outlays for equipment of $82,000.

Your Company's Cash Flow Statement

Place your company's cash flow statement here.

_____(COMPANY NAME)
CASH FLOW STATEMENT
YEAR END 20____

Operating $(000's)

Net profit

Add: Depreciation   _____
        Decrease in inventories   _____
        Decrease in fixed assets   _____
        Increase in notes payable   _____
        Increase in long-term debt   _____

Minus: Increase in accounts receivable   _____
        Increase in prepaid expenses   _____
        Increased foreign receipts   _____
        Decrease in accounts payable   _____
        Decrease in accrued expenses   _____
        Decrease in accrued taxes   _____

Total cash from operations

Investing
Total cash from investing   _____

Financing
Total cash from financing   _____

Increase in cash and marketable securities _____

The Statement of Retained Earnings

The statement of retained earnings reports how much of the firm's earnings were not paid out in dividends. It shows the changes in the common equity between balance sheet dates.

JOG CORPORATION STATEMENT OF RETAINED EARNINGS YEAR END 20XX	
Balance of retained earnings, end of year 1	$3,080,000
Add net income, end of year 2	1,512,000
Total retained earnings	4,592,000
Minus dividends paid	(500,000)
Retained earnings, end of year 2	4,092,000

_____(COMPANY NAME) STATEMENT OF RETAINED EARNINGS YEAR END 20___	
Balance of retained earnings, end of year 1	_____
Add net income, end of year 2	_____
Total retained earnings	_____
Minus dividends paid	_____
Retained earnings, end of year 2	_____

Checklist

Did you...

- ❏ remember that a balance sheet describes the financial condition of a company as of a particular date?

- ❏ remember to begin your analysis by examining the major categories?

- ❏ remember the definition of a safe company?

- ❏ make the connection between net worth and shareholders' equity?

- ❏ note that the statement of retained earnings contains the retained earnings and dividends paid?

- ❏ remember that there is a difference between the profit reported on the income statement and the cash shown on the balance sheet?

- ❏ remember that cash is generated when there is an increase in a liability and/or a decrease in an asset, and cash flows out when there is a decrease in a liability and/or an increase in an asset?

- ❏ use the cash flow statement to help determine where the company generated cash and what it did with it?

- ❏ remember that the statement of cash flow reports the impact of a company's operating, investing, and financing activities on the cash flow over an accounting period?

- ❏ remember that the statement of retained earnings reports how much of the company's earnings were not paid out in dividends? *Those not paid out to shareholders are "retained" inside the company.*

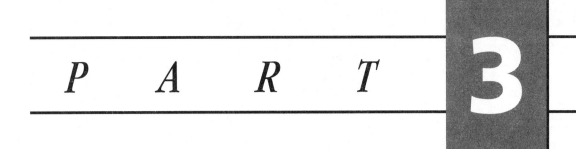

P A R T 3

Asset

Management

Management of Current Assets

The current assets presented in this part of the book are accounts receivable and inventory.

Current assets are important to every business no matter how large or small. They pay the bills that flow in from purchases of raw materials, wages, rent, etc. Without sufficient current assets, a company cannot survive. The cash account and the marketable securities account contain all the "real" money a business has. True, accounts receivable presumably will be paid—but as of the date of the balance sheet, they have not been. The inventory may or may not be sold for the amount shown on the balance sheet; only time will tell. For service businesses, inventory is probably not a factor. *Remember, "current" means in one year or less.*

Managing Receivables Policy

Let's look at what might happen if JOG Corporation tries to increase sales by easing its credit policy. Let's assume that all sales made by JOG Corporation are credit sales. The company has no cash sales.

If sales rise, so will expenses. Labor, material, cost of financing or carrying the extra credit, and probably bad debts will increase. The question is, will it be worth the expense to ease the restrictions on granting credit as a means to gain higher sales? Nothing else will be changed—advertising will be the same, so will the sales force and the equipment.

The things that must be considered are:

➤ Projected additional sales

➤ Discounts for early payment: 2% if paid within 10 days

➤ Increase in late payments (what percentage of sales and for what length of time)

➤ Increase in inventory (and all associated costs)

➤ Where to finance (equity or debt)

➤ Whether there is excess manufacturing capacity (and trained operators)

➤ Opportunity costs (the loss of other areas to use debt or equity)

➤ Increase in bad debts (what percentage of sales)

In the example on page 41, operating expenses as a percent of sales are held constant (which may not always happen). Even so, the increase in bad debt, the carrying of receivables, the credit operations, and allowing a discount to encourage faster payment caused a drop in income of 1.5% of sales. This equates to $465,000 in sales.

	Projected Income: Old Policy $(000's)	% of Sales	Effect of Policy Change $(000's)	Projected Income: New Policy $(000's)	% of Sales
JOG CORPORATION **PROJECTED ANALYSIS OF CREDIT POLICY ON ACCOUNTS RECEIVABLE PROFIT** **END OF YEAR 3**					
Sales	25,000	100.0	6,000	31,000	100.0
Cost of goods sold	16,000	64.0	3,840	19,840	64.0
Gross profit before discounts	9,000	36.0	2,160	11,160	36.0
Minus discounts	0	0	372	372	1.2
Gross profits	9,000	36.0	1,788	10,788	34.8
Operating expenses	5,250	21.0	1,260	6,510	21.0
Profit before credit costs and taxes	3,750	15.0	528	4,278	13.8
Credit operation expenses	250	1.0	(157)	93	0.3
Cost of carrying receivables	210	0.8	120	330	1.1
Bad debt losses	100	0.4	520	620	2.0
Profit before taxes	3,190	12.8	45	3,235	10.4
Taxes (at 35%)	1,116	4.5	16	1,132	3.6
Net income	2,074	8.3	29	2,103	6.8

JOG Corporation Notes

Discounts are 2% if paid within 10 days. It is estimated that 60% of the customers will take them.

$31,000,000 × 60 × .02 = $372,000

It is also estimated that 20% of the customers will pay on time (30-40 days), 18% will pay late (over 40 days), and 2% will not pay (up from 0.4%). The cost of credit operations will be reduced, because of less emphasis on checking references and lax receivables collection.

Let's tabulate the information we have:

	Year 3 $(000's)	
	Old Policy	New Policy
1. Net sales (see page 41)	25,000	31,000
2. Percent of sales outstanding at year end	15%	25%
3. Accounts receivable		
4. Beginning of year	3,233	3,233
5. End of year (Line 1 x Line 2)	3,750	7,750
6. Average A/R (Line 4 + Line 5)/2	3,492	5,492

Let's calculate the turnover of receivables. It measures how fast receivables are being collected. Usually the higher the ratio, the better. Last year, the ratio was 7.1 times. The way to determine the ratio is to divide the net sales by the average accounts receivable.

Under the old policy:

$$\frac{\$25,000,000}{\$3,492,000} = 7.2 \text{ times}$$

Under the new policy:

$$\frac{\$31,000,000}{\$5,492,000} = 5.6 \text{ times}$$

Last year's average collection period for accounts receivable was 51 days. The average collection period is determined by dividing the turnover of receivables into 365 days. It calculates the average number of days it takes to collect receivables. If nothing else changes, the expected average will be 51 days.

Under the new policy the average will jump to 65 days. In general, the lower the average collection period, the better.

JOG Corporation currently has a turnover of 7.1 times, or 51 days to collect. The expected increase to 7.2 times (51 days) is nearly identical to last year. But under the new policy it falls to 5.6 times, or 65 days. This is a trend in the wrong direction. Even though the company has a high liquidity position, this may not be the best way for it to invest the shareholders' money.

Perhaps JOG Corporation would be better off to concentrate on spending a little more time and money collecting its current receivables, instead of trying to increase sales by increasing receivables. Remember, it's the cash that is collected, not the sales made, that counts.

Variable costs are 60% and the cost of funds to the corporation is 10%. Only variable expenses are considered because there will be no purchase of equipment to support the increase in sales.

The cost of carrying receivables is determined by:

Average accounts receivable x Variable cost ratio x Cost of funds

$3,492,000 x .60 x .10 = $209,520

$5,492,000 x .60 x .10 = $329,520

The projected analysis allows us to assess the effects of our policy without trial and error. However, these projected statements are based on assumptions that may turn out to be incorrect. A manager must use experience and judgment along with these indicators.

The figure for average accounts receivable can be misleading if taken from an annual report, where management normally strives to make a good showing.

Depending on the industry, accounts receivable will vary during the business cycle. A corporation will usually end its fiscal year at the end of its business cycle—when the corporation is in a high cash position and has low accounts receivable (and low inventory, which is discussed in the next section). For example, a corporation which experiences high sales during the December holiday season will likely end its fiscal year as soon as possible after collecting outstanding receivables. This methodology maximizes fourth quarter sales and minimizes outstanding receivables.

Projected Analysis for Your Company

It is very difficult to evaluate changes in the credit policy for large businesses. Below are some questions you can ask yourself to help determine if a proposed change would be beneficial to your company.

Write the figures for your company in the spaces below:

Projected sales $_____

Discounts $_____

Increase in late payments _____ %

Increase in inventory $_____

Where to finance: Debt? ❏   Equity? ❏

Is there excess manufacturing or other required capacity?   Yes ❏   No ❏

Any lost opportunity costs?   Yes ❏   No ❏

Have they been evaluated?   Yes ❏   No ❏

Results _____

_____

_____

_____

Will there be an increase in bad debts?   Yes ❏   No ❏

If yes, by how much? $_____

What percentage increase?   _____ %

Will credit operation expenses rise or fall?   Rise ❏   Fall ❏

By how much? $_____ or _____ %

Will cost of carrying receivables rise?   Yes ❏   No ❏

By how much? $_____ or _____ %

Calculations

Average accounts receivable = Accounts receivable (beginning of the accounting period) + Accounts receivable (end of the accounting period) divided by 2.

Current policy:

$$\frac{\$ \underline{\hspace{3cm}} + \$ \underline{\hspace{3cm}}}{2} = \$ \underline{\hspace{3cm}}$$

New policy:

$$\frac{\$ \underline{\hspace{3cm}} + \$ \underline{\hspace{3cm}}}{2} = \$ \underline{\hspace{3cm}}$$

Turnover of receivables = $\dfrac{\text{Annual sales}}{\text{Average accounts receivable}}$

Current policy:

$$\frac{\$ \underline{\hspace{2cm}}}{\$ \underline{\hspace{2cm}}} = \$ \underline{\hspace{3cm}}$$

New policy:

$$\frac{\$ \underline{\hspace{2cm}}}{\$ \underline{\hspace{2cm}}} = \$ \underline{\hspace{3cm}}$$

Cost of carrying receivables = Average accounts receivable x Variable cost ratio x Cost of funds. The variable cost ratio is determined from your company's expenses. The cost of funds is determined by your company.

Current policy:

$\$ \underline{\hspace{2cm}}$ x $\underline{\hspace{2cm}} \%$ x $\underline{\hspace{2cm}} \%$ = $\$ \underline{\hspace{2cm}}$

New policy:

$\$ \underline{\hspace{2cm}}$ x $\underline{\hspace{2cm}} \%$ x $\underline{\hspace{2cm}} \%$ = $\$ \underline{\hspace{2cm}}$

Inventory Valuation Methods

In this section we will look at ways of valuing the inventory through the accounting techniques of the average cost method, FIFO (first-in-first-out), and LIFO (last-in-first-out).

The Average Cost Method

To determine average cost, divide the total number of units of goods available for sale into the total purchase cost for the period of time under examination. The total purchase cost should include freight-in and delivery charges to get the raw material to the manufacturer or the goods to the supplier. The total number of goods that have been sold during this period multiplied by the same average cost would equate to the cost of goods sold.

Example: Three items are in inventory. If the first item cost $100, the second cost $300, and the third cost $500, what is the average cost of goods sold? If two of these units are sold, what is the average remaining inventory valuation?

The average purchase cost would be:

$$\frac{\$100 + \$300 + \$500}{3} = \frac{\$900}{3} = \$300$$

So the cost of goods sold is $300 × 2 = $600. The remaining inventory valuation is $300.

FIFO

The FIFO (first-in-first-out) method is based on the assumption that the inventory first acquired is the first used or sold. Therefore, the remaining inventory consists of the most recently purchased items. This method will reflect the most recent cost of the inventory on a balance sheet. The cost of goods sold will reflect the earliest cost of purchases.

Example: Three items are in inventory. The first to be purchased cost $100, the second $300, and the third $500. What is the cost of goods sold? If two of these items are sold, what is the value of the remaining inventory?

The cost of goods sold is $100 + $300 = $400. The value of the remaining inventory is $500.

LIFO

The LIFO (last-in-first-out) method is based on the assumption that the inventory last acquired is the first used or sold. Therefore, the remaining inventory consists of the oldest or first purchased items. This method will reflect the earliest cost of the inventory on the balance sheet. The cost of goods sold will reflect the most recent prices.

Example: The same three items are in inventory. The cost of the first item to be purchased was $100, the cost of the second $300, and the cost of the third $500. What is the cost of goods sold? If two of these items are sold, what is the value of the remaining inventory?

The cost of goods sold is $500 + $300 = $800. The remaining inventory is valued at $100.

A corporation selects the inventory method which reduces tax liability. From the following example, we see that during a period of rising prices (reflected in the cost of goods sold), LIFO would reduce the corporation's tax liability and FIFO would increase it.

Inventory Valuation Methods (CONTINUED)

	Average Cost Method	FIFO	LIFO
Beginning inventory	$10,000	$10,000	$10,000
Purchases	12,000	12,000	12,000
Goods for sale	22,000	22,000	22,000
Sales	15,000	15,000	15,000
Cost of goods sold	11,000	10,000	12,000
Ending inventory (goods for sale less cost of goods sold)	11,000	12,000	10,000
Profit (sales less cost of goods sold)	4,000	5,000	3,000
Taxes (at 35%)	1,400	1,750	1,050
Net earnings	2,600	3,250	1,950

In this example, it is assumed that the average cost method provides the best measure of performance. In a period of declining prices, FIFO would reduce the corporation's tax payments and LIFO would increase them–provided the government doesn't change the tax laws to reflect inflation. (Although different methods are preferable under specific economic conditions, it should be noted that inventory methods, once established, cannot be changed without IRS approval.)

The average cost method will probably provide the most accurate measure of inventory valuation. It treats all inventory alike. If your company has 10,000 items in inventory, each has a distinct purpose, shelf life, and sales rate; and each should be treated individually in order to keep the correct amounts available.

Valuing Your Company's Inventory

Fill in the figures for your company:

	Average Cost Method	FIFO	LIFO
Beginning inventory	_____	_____	_____
Purchases	_____	_____	_____
Goods for sale	_____	_____	_____
Sales	_____	_____	_____
Cost of goods sold	_____	_____	_____
Ending inventory (goods for sale less cost of goods sold)	_____	_____	_____
Profit (sales less cost of goods sold)	_____	_____	_____
Taxes (at 35%)	_____	_____	_____
Net earnings	_____	_____	_____

Which method gives the most realistic earnings for your company?

❏ Average Cost Method   ❏ FIFO   ❏ LIFO

Why? _____

_____

Depreciation

This section covers one aspect of fixed asset valuation called depreciation. *Depreciation* is a noncash expense which allocates the cost of capital equipment to periods into the future. *Remember, capital assets are often referred to as fixed or long-term assets and are assets which will be of use to the company for more than one year.* Both buildings and equipment wear out or become technologically obsolete; depreciation provides a means of writing off the costs of these assets over their remaining useful life.

From a financial point of view, depreciation is a source of cash because depreciation is an expense which reduces taxes. It is the process of allocating asset cost over future accounting periods. A reduction of the value of a fixed asset through depreciation reduces assets and shareholders' equity on the balance sheet.

Depreciation appears on the income statement as an expense. It is usually included in cost of goods sold or in administrative expenses, depending on whether or not the asset is used in manufacturing. *Remember: depreciation is a noncash expense.*

There are two main ways of calculating depreciation for book accounting purposes: the straight-line method and the accelerated methods.

Straight-Line Method

The simplest and most common way to depreciate an asset is the straight-line method. To use it, divide the estimated useful life of an asset into its purchase price minus any salvage or resale value. Salvage or resale value is the estimated amount a company can expect to receive from the sale of the asset at the end of its useful life.

Example: A piece of equipment has a useful life of five years. It cost $6,000 and it has a resale value of $1,000 at the end of its useful life. What is the yearly depreciation?

Subtract the $1,000 resale price from the $6,000 cost. Divide the remaining $5,000 by five years. The depreciation is $1,000 per year for the next five years. This amounts to 20% per year. In three years the accumulated (total to date) depreciation would be $3,000.

Accelerated Methods

Many fixed assets are more valuable in their earlier years than in their later years. This is due to technical obsolescence or a decline in mechanical efficiency. Accelerated depreciation attempts to reflect this value by allowing greater depreciation in the early years.

The two most common accelerated methods are the double declining balance method and the sum-of-the-years'-digits method. The effect of both is to write off approximately two-thirds of the cost in the first half of the asset's estimated life. (The straight-line method would write off equal parts each year.)

The Double Declining Balance Method

The double declining balance method uses a book value (cost less accumulated depreciation) rather than the original cost to figure the depreciation. In the straight-line method the salvage or resale value was subtracted, but in the double declining balance method it is not. A depreciation of 40% per year, or double the straight-line method's 20% per year, is applied to the book value.

Example: We start with a value of $6,000. In the first year, we deduct 40%, or $2,400. In the second year, the book value is $3,600 ($6,000 – 2,400 = $3,600). Again, we deduct 40%, or $1,440. In the third year, we deduct 40% of the remaining book value of $2,160 ($3,600 – 1,440 = $2,160), or $864.

An asset cannot be depreciated below its salvage value. So, beginning with the fourth year, the depreciation is the remaining book value of $1,296 minus the salvage value of $1,000 divided by the number of years of useful life remaining. The $296 depreciation is divided equally over the last two years, at $148 per year.

The Sum-of-the-Years'-Digits Method

The sum-of-the-years'-digits method uses the original cost less the salvage value. The years of useful life are added together. In the above example, we had five years of useful life, so we add $1 + 2 + 3 + 4 + 5 = 15$. The depreciation is number of years of depreciation remaining divided by the sum-of-the-years'-digits. In this case, depreciation is 5/15 the first year, 4/15 the second year, 3/15 the third year, and so on.

Thus, for the first year, depreciation is 5/15 of $5,000, or $1,667. For the second year, 4/15 of $5,000 is $1,333. For the third year, 3/15 is $1,000. For the fourth year, 2/15 is $667. For the last year, 1/15 is $333. This adds up to the original purchase price less the salvage value ($6,000 − 1,000 = $5,000).

The following table compares the three depreciation methods for an asset that cost $6,000, has a salvage value of $1,000 and has five years of useful life.

Year	Straight-Line	Double Declining Balance	Sum-of-the-Years'-Digits
1	$1,000	$2,400	$1,667
2	1,000	1,440	1,333
3	1,000	864	1,000
4	1,000	148*	667
5	1,000	148*	333

*Salvage value of $1,000 subtracted and last two years split equally.

Review

For each statement below, indicate whether **A** or **B** is correct. Put a check (✔) in the appropriate box.

1. Current assets are important because

    ❏ A. they pay the bills.

    ❏ B. they look good on a balance sheet.

2. An important item to consider when changing credit policy is

    ❏ A. the amount spent on advertising.

    ❏ B. projected additional sales.

3. The method to determine the turnover of accounts receivable is

    ❏ A. divide total credit sales by average receivables.

    ❏ B. multiply credit sales by accounts receivable.

4. Accounts receivable are

    ❏ A. better than cash.

    ❏ B. one part of current assets.

5. In determining the effect of a new credit policy to increase sales, only variable expenses are considered because

    ❏ A. they are the only kind a corporation has.

    ❏ B. fixed expenses are usually not affected by an increase in sales.

Answers: 1. A, 2. B, 3. A, 4. B, 5. B

For each statement below, circle **T** if you think it is true, or **F** if you think it is false.

1. If we do the statements correctly, we don't have to worry about having good judgment. **T** **F**

2. The balance sheet, income statement, and analysis of credit projections are always totally accurate for every corporation. **T** **F**

3. FIFO is a type of federal tax. **T** **F**

4. The average cost method usually provides the best measure of performance. **T** **F**

5. During rising prices, LIFO would reduce reported income. **T** **F**

6. Depreciation is a noncash expense. **T** **F**

7. The straight-line method of depreciation is complex and seldom used. **T** **F**

8. Accelerated methods allow more depreciation to be taken in the early years of an equipment's life cycle. **T** **F**

Answers: 1. F, 2. F, 3. F, 4. F, 5. T, 6. T, 7. F, 8. T

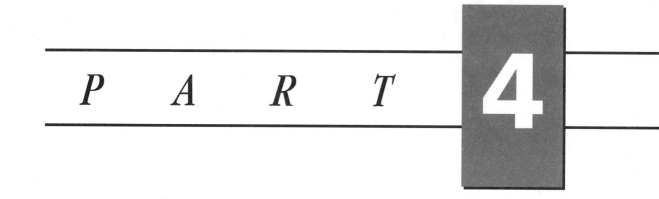

New Ratios

Ratios Help Make Decisions

Corporate financial statements (unlike those for partnerships and sole proprietorships) include capital stock. The management of the corporation must report to its owners—the common shareholders—how the company is doing.

One of the techniques used is capital stock ratios. Management must also exercise care in the handling of debt, and the use of ratios helps them do this.

This part of the book introduces ratios that will help a manager make decisions regarding the use of debt and equity. There are five equity ratios and one additional debt ratio that help gauge the amount of interest payments covered by the earnings.

Capital Stock/Market Ratios

In the process of starting a business, all of the money from the sale of stock would be shown under "Shareholders' equity" as paid-in capital or common stock, and under "Current assets" as cash. If the corporation is ongoing, there will probably be some amount in "Retained earnings."

The value of a share of stock is the amount a buyer is willing to pay for it. For companies listed on a stock exchange, this is the market value. Several factors make up this price. Those looking for income would be interested in the dividends paid; those looking for future growth would be interested in future earnings, often called *capital gains*.

Capital stock or market ratios are:

➤ **Return on equity:** indicates the return on the shareholder's investment,

➤ **Price-earnings ratio:** is used to determine the amount potential investors are willing to pay before investing,

➤ **Capitalization rate:** is the reciprocal of the price-earnings ratio; it measures the rate of return the market demands,

➤ **Earnings per share ratio:** measures the earnings for each share of common stock; this is the amount available to each stockholder if management chooses to pay it all out, and

➤ **Dividend yield:** is the relationship between cash dividends paid to common shareholders and the market price per share of common stock.

Note: The following is an introduction to five capital stock or market ratios. This initial discussion does not provide sufficient tools for investment decision making. It is an introduction only and readers are advised to seek additional information prior to making investments in any company.

The next page shows JOG Corporation's balance sheet and income statement. The ratios will be calculated using the figures from these statements.

JOG CORPORATION
BALANCE SHEET
YEAR END 20XX

Current Assets	$(000's)	Current Liabilities	$(000's)
Cash	1,270	Notes payable	500
Gov't securities	407	Accts payable	408
Accts receivable	3,233	Accrued expenses	449
Inventories		Accrued taxes	500
Finished merch	3,300	Total current liabilities	1,857
Work in process	775		
Raw mtl/supplies	315	**Long-term Debt**	
Goods in transit	175	15-year notes	1,150
	4,565	10-year notes	1,000
Total current assets	9,475	Total long-term debt	2,150
Property and Equipment			
Land	482	**Shareholders' Equity**	
Buildings	418	Capital stock $1 par	
Equipment	1,157	value (2,500,000 auth)	
	2,057	1,033,000 outstanding	1,033
Depreciation	903		
Total fixed assets	1,154	Paid-in capital	2,167
Other Assets		Retained earnings	4,092
Prepaid expenses	114	Total shareholders'	
Foreign receipts	556	equity	7,292
Total other assets	670	**Total liabilities**	
Total assets	**11,299**	**and equity**	**11,299**

JOG CORPORATION – INCOME STATEMENT
YEAR END 20XX

Net sales	$21,108,000
Cost of goods sold	13,546,000
Gross profit	7,562,000
Operating expenses	4,958,000
Earnings before interest & taxes	2,604,000
Interest charges	278,000
Earnings before taxes	2,326,000
Income taxes (35%)	814,000
Net earnings	1,512,000
Retained earnings at the beginning of the year	3,080,000
	4,592,000
Dividends paid	500,000
Retained earnings at the end of the year	$ 4,092,000
Shares of common stock outstanding	1,033,000
Current price per share	$10.00

Return on Equity

The *return on equity (ROE)* ratio measures the return on the shareholders' investment. It indicates how well management is utilizing the owners' investment.

$$\text{Return on equity} \;=\; \frac{\text{Net earnings}}{\text{Shareholders' equity}} \;=\; \frac{\$1,512,000}{\$7,292,000} \;=\; 20.7\%$$

A low ratio means the owners or investors could have made more money investing in something else. For example, if an investor could earn over 21% on another investment, the investor might consider moving his or her money out of JOG Corporation. This would depend on the perceived risk of the other investment. However, this ratio should be considered in the light of what has happened during the business cycle, such as expansion, taking on debt, or changes in the economy.

A high ratio means management has done well (or they are hiding something until after the annual report). In general, the higher the better.

This ratio is related to the *return on assets* (ROA) when it is modified by an operating ratio and the equity multiplier. It will change due to variance in the turnover of operating assets, operating profit, and the equity multiplier.* (EBIT is *earnings before interest and taxes*, also called operating profit on some income statements.)

$$
\begin{array}{ccccc}
\text{Return on assets} & \times & \text{Operating ratio} & \times & \text{Equity multiplier} \\[2mm]
= \dfrac{\text{EBIT}}{\text{Total assets}} & \times & \dfrac{\text{Net earnings}}{\text{EBIT}} & \times & \dfrac{\text{Total assets}}{\text{Shareholders' equity}} \\[4mm]
= \dfrac{\$2,604,000}{\$11,299,000} & \times & \dfrac{\$1,512,000}{\$2,604,000} & \times & \dfrac{\$11,299,000}{\$7,292,000} \\[4mm]
= \quad .23 & \times & .58 & \times & 1.6 \quad = \; 21\%
\end{array}
$$

* It is called an equity multiplier because debt is also used to finance the assets, but it all belongs to the shareholders.

Earnings Per Share Ratio

The *earnings per share ratio (EPS)*, or book value ratio, measures management's success in achieving profits for the owners. This is the amount available to the common shareholder after the payment of all charges and taxes for the accounting period.

$$\text{Earnings per share ratio} = \frac{\text{Net earnings}}{\text{Number of common shares outstanding}} = \frac{\$1,512,000}{1,033,000} = \$1.46$$

A low ratio means the management is not performing well with regard to earnings. Either limited net earnings due to sluggish sales or high costs and/or a large number of common shares outstanding. Start-up companies or those with many products still in development generally have low earnings per share, if any.

A high ratio means the stock has a high rate of return. Such a stock will generally sell at a higher multiple of its book value than a stock with a low rate of return. Mature companies and/or those with limited shares of common stock outstanding generally have high ratios.

The usefulness of this ratio is questionable. There is little or no relationship between book value (based on historical costs) and market value (based on future earning and dividends). This ratio is very dependent on the economy in general, the specific industry, the age of the company, and the number of shares of common stock outstanding.

Common stockholders generally consider a decrease in earnings per share to be unfavorable. A decline in EPS can indicate a decline in the profitability of a company and raises concerns about its future growth and profitability. Alternately, an increase in EPS is considered positive as long as the increase keeps up with market expectations.

Some analysts use this ratio in connection with one called the market to book value ratio. It looks like this:

$$\frac{\text{Market price per share}}{\text{Book value per share}}$$

This ratio tells if the market price is higher than book value and by how many times, or if it is lower and by what percent.

Price/Earnings Ratio

The *price/earnings ratio (P/E)* measures how much the investors are willing to pay per dollar of reported profits.

$$\text{Price/earnings ratio} \;=\; \frac{\text{Market price per share}}{\text{Earnings per share}} \;=\; \frac{\$10.00}{\$1.46} \;=\; 6.8 \text{ times}$$

At the current earnings rate an investor "gets" his money in 6.8 years, either in dividends or in increased book value, if not market value. Sometimes called the *multiple* that the market places on the earnings of the company.

A low ratio means the investors are not willing to pay very much for a share of stock (market perception that the company will have minimal future earnings growth). The potential shareholders consider the company to be risky. However, if an investor wants this stock and believes it will grow, the lower the ratio the better for that investor. A low ratio could also mean that a good market has not been developed for this stock.

A high ratio means the investors believe that the company has a high future earnings or high growth potential, other things being equal. But if the ratio is too high, investors may look for something more reasonable.

This ratio and the others in this section provide an indication to management of what the investors think about the corporation—its current, past, and future performance. Generally, if all the ratios are showing good, steady performance, the stock price will be high.

The P/E ratio is a commonly used ratio for evaluating a company today. The P/E ratio of most stocks has varied widely in recent years ranging from a low of about 10 to a high of over 100. The outlook for future earnings is the major factor influencing a company's P/E ratio.

The P/E ratio is used to compare companies within the same business sector or that are similar in nature. By using this ratio, investors can determine which company within an industry may offer the best investment opportunities. For instance, the P/E ratios for two automobile manufacturers are 15 and 18 respectively. Assuming that the companies have similar future earnings potential, an investment in the company with the lower P/E ratio of 15 will generate greater *future* earnings potential for an investor.

The P/E ratios for many publicly traded companies are given in the business section of most daily newspapers. Remember that since the price of stocks can change daily, the P/E ratio will change daily as well.

Capitalization Rate

The *capitalization rate*, or rate of return ratio, measures the rate of return that the market demands for the corporation. As the price/earnings ratio increases, the capitalization rate decreases.

Note*: The capitalization rate is the reciprocal of the price/earnings ratio.*

$$\text{Capitalization rate} \ = \ \frac{\text{Earnings per share}}{\text{Market price per share}} \ = \ \frac{\$1.46}{\$10.00} \ = \ 14.6\%$$

A low ratio means the investors don't demand a very high return on their money because they consider the corporation to be a good investment.

A high ratio means the investors want a high return for each dollar invested. In other words it takes a large payoff to attract investors.

Corporations which have high earnings growth generally have high prices in relation to earnings, and vice versa. The capitalization rate reports this in terms of a percentage return based on the selling price of a share of stock and the amount that the corporation earned on that share.

Dividend Yield

The *dividend yield* measures the relationship between cash dividends paid to common shareholders and the market price per share of common stock.

$$\text{Dividend yield} \ = \ \frac{\text{Dividends per share}}{\text{Market price per share}} \ = \ \frac{\$ .48}{\$10.00} \ = \ 4.8\%$$

A low ratio means a low rate of current income distributions, or return, on the stock investment. An investor could possibly increase his or her return by selling the stock and purchasing stock in a higher yielding company.

A high ratio indicates a favorable return. As long as dividend yield remains high, an investor would have no incentive to change his or her investment.

Dividends are of importance to shareholders who rely on corporate dividends for regular cash income. In general, the higher the dividend yield, the lower the capital gain expectations through rising stock price.

Investors respond negatively when a company reduces its dividends. Generally a reduced dividend payout is followed by a decline in the market price per share of stock.

This ratio is best used to compare companies with relatively stable stock prices for two reasons. First, a company with a wildly fluctuating stock price does not provide as meaningful a yield ratio. Second, these types of stocks are intended for long-term returns, not the increase in capital gains.

Debt Coverage Ratios

Debt coverage ratios provide indications of a company's vulnerability to risk. The debt to equity ratio (presented in Part 1) and the ratio shown below provide the necessary tools to evaluate the corporation's safety.

The *times interest earned ratio* measures the extent that operating income can decline before the firm is unable to meet its annual interest charges.

$$\text{Times interest earned ratio} = \frac{\text{Earnings before interest and taxes (EBIT)}}{\text{Interest}} = \frac{\$2,604,000}{\$278,000} = 9.4 \text{ times}$$

The generally accepted standard depends on the industry, but 6 or 7 times is a good target to shoot for.

A low ratio means a low margin of safety. The company may have difficulty borrowing.

A high ratio means the company probably has borrowing capacity.

A variation of this ratio is to add noncash charges such as depreciation, amortization, and depletion to net earnings for cash flow coverage.

$$\frac{\text{Net earnings} + \text{Depreciation}}{\text{Interest}} = \frac{\$1,512,000 + \$82,000}{\$278,000}$$

$$= 5.7 \text{ times}$$

Other fixed charges that must be paid to stay in business, such as rent, should be added to the interest payments.

Another variation is called the *fixed charge coverage*. This ratio recognizes that many companies lease assets and sometimes incur long-term obligations through the lease agreements. If your corporation uses or is beginning to use leasing, this ratio may make more sense than the times interest earned ratio.

It looks like this:

$$\text{Fixed charge coverage} = \frac{\text{EBIT} + \text{lease payments}}{\text{Interest charges} + \text{lease payments}}$$

Limitations of Ratio Use

Ratios are more useful for small, focused companies and fairly autonomous divisions of large corporations. Ratios don't tell too much about a consolidated statement of a large multinational corporation. It is difficult if not impossible to calculate a ratio for a particular business segment which is part of a larger corporation because financial information is presented as consolidated data. You will have to use your judgment to select comparable companies for evaluation purposes and recognize that the comparisons are estimates at best.

Ratios are no substitute for insight, judgment, and objective thinking. A company may change over time, making past ratios of doubtful value. Also, comparing companies of different ages is not very meaningful. Likewise, seasonal factors, unexpected disasters, or windfall profits can greatly distort ratios and make comparisons difficult.

Other things which can distort ratios are different means of accounting for expenses such as inventory and/or depreciation methods, the fact that a company may be making a lot of money from investments rather than its own operations, and a particular company's strategic plans—they may want to have low profitability now as they are building for the future. And leasing, renting, borrowing, and payment practices can make ratios look good for this accounting period but not the next.

Ratios should always be compared to those of other firms in the same industry. This can be done fairly easily, as several companies publish comparative ratio analyses. Published industry averages are available on the Internet or at your public library. Don't forget that companies within a given industry segment can vary widely within those industry norms.

Remember that ratios are ballpark estimates. Ratios cannot consistently provide complete, detailed, and accurate data. If they could, we wouldn't need good management.

The main benefit of ratios is to track trends from one accounting period to the next.

Review

For each statement below, circle **T** if you think it is true, or **F** if you think it is false.

1. The return on equity ratio measures the return on the shareholder's investment. T F

2. The corporation's management wants earnings per share to be high. T F

3. The price/earnings ratio measures how much investors are willing to pay per dollar of reported profits. T F

4. The price/earnings ratio is sometimes called the capitalization ratio. T F

5. A high times interest earned ratio is not good for the creditors of the corporation. T F

6. Ratios are more useful for small, focused companies than large, diverse corporations. T F

7. By using ratios you don't need good business judgment. T F

8. Better comparisons of corporate ratios are made if the corporations are in the same industry. T F

Answers: 1. T, 2. T, 3. T, 4. T, 5. F, 6. T, 7. F, 8. T

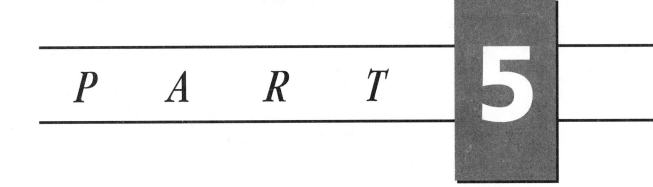

PART 5

The Interaction
of Ratios

How Ratios Affect Each Other

If one ratio is changed, chances are another will be affected. Therefore it is important to look at all affected ratios. By doing this, you can see on paper what would happen to your total business if a particular ratio changed. Then you can decide whether you want to take steps to make the new ratio happen.

Changes will also occur during the course of doing business. These changes may be good or not so good. Ratios help track and determine what is causing these changes.

This part of the book describes some of the ways to evaluate changes through ratio analysis, and to understand what might happen to other ratios if we cause one to look good. The ratios are the liquidity, profitability, and efficiency ratios from Part 1 and the times interest earned ratio from Part 4.

The ratios are:

$$\frac{\text{Current assets}}{\text{Current liabilities}} \qquad \frac{\text{Net earnings before taxes}}{\text{Total assets}}$$

$$\frac{\text{Total debt}}{\text{Shareholders' equity}} \qquad \frac{\text{EBIT}}{\text{Net sales}}$$

$$\frac{\text{EBIT}}{\text{Interest}} \qquad \frac{\text{Net sales}}{\text{Average inventory}}$$

$$\frac{\text{Accounts receivable} \times 365}{\text{Net sales}} \qquad \frac{\text{Net sales}}{\text{Total assets}}$$

$$\frac{\text{Net earnings before taxes}}{\text{Shareholders' equity}} \qquad \frac{\text{Fixed assets}}{\text{Shareholders' equity}}$$

$$\frac{\text{Net sales}}{\text{Working capital}}$$

Notes:

➤ **EBIT** = **E**arnings **B**efore **I**nterest and **T**axes

➤ Net earnings before taxes and EBIT over Net Sales will be considered as one ratio rather than two for this exercise.

How Ratios Affect Each Other (CONTINUED)

There are five* ratios that have net sales as either the numerator or denominator, three ratios that have net earnings before taxes as the numerator, and three that have shareholders' equity as the denominator.

If one part of a ratio is changed and that part appears in another ratio, that other ratio will change also. For example, one of the most used indicators is the return on investment ratio. Suppose the net earnings before taxes or EBIT (earnings before interest and taxes) is $2,000, and the shareholders' equity is $10,000.

$$\text{Return on investment ratio} = \frac{\text{Net earnings before taxes (EBIT)}}{\text{Shareholders' equity}} = \frac{\$2,000}{\$10,000} = 20\%$$

If you want to increase this ratio to 30%, you can either increase profits by increasing prices or sales, lowering expenses, or lower the shareholders' equity by increasing liabilities or reducing assets. Either

$$\frac{\$3,000}{\$10,000} = 30\% \quad \text{or} \quad \frac{\$2,000}{\$6,000} = 30\%$$

What happens to the other ratios when prices are raised or expenses lowered? Two other ratios are affected:

$$\text{Rate of return on sales} = \frac{\text{Net earnings before taxes (EBIT)}}{\text{Net sales}} = \text{higher}$$

$$\text{Rate of return on assets} = \frac{\text{Net earnings before taxes (EBIT)}}{\text{Total assets}} = \text{higher}$$

Generally if these ratios are higher the company would receive a better return on sales and a better return on assets.

---

* Two ratios are treated as one for this exercise: the net earnings before taxes over net sales ratio and the EBIT over net sales ratio.

What if shareholders' equity drops? Two other ratios are affected.

$$\text{Debt to equity ratio} \ = \ \frac{\text{Total debt}}{\text{Shareholders' equity}} \ = \ \text{higher}$$

$$\text{Fixed assets to equity ratio} \ = \ \frac{\text{Fixed assets}}{\text{Shareholders' equity}} \ = \ \text{higher}$$

In this case, higher is not better. It shows that debt increased as a percentage of equity and that fixed assets increased as a part of shareholders' equity. This means that the shareholders' equity is less liquid and more is tied up in fixed assets.

These are the exercises to go through when trying to change the ratio. A change in one ratio may not be good for the business, or it may call for a less drastic change to be made in order to maintain a balance.

Another example is a change in net sales. Suppose the net earnings before taxes is $2,000 and the net sales are $20,000.

$$\text{Rate of return on sales} \ = \ \frac{\text{Net earnings before tax (EBIT)}}{\text{Net sales}} \ = \ \frac{\$2,000}{\$20,000} \ = \ 10\%$$

Say that you want to raise this ratio to 20%. You could either double the profit from the same sales, or you could cut the sales in half! (In reality, it is highly unlikely that you could support the same profit on half the sales. But we'll go through this as an exercise.)

How Ratios Affect Each Other (CONTINUED)

If the net earnings before interest and tax (EBIT) is doubled or the net sales halved, two ratios will be affected.

EBIT responds like the original ratio:

$$\frac{\text{EBIT}}{\text{Net sales}} \quad = \quad \text{higher}$$

Accounts receivable turnover is higher, which is not good.

$$\frac{\text{Accounts receivable} \times 365}{\text{Net sales}} \quad = \quad \text{higher}$$

If the net sales are reduced, three other ratios will be affected.

The investment turnover ratio is lower, which is not good.

$$\frac{\text{Net sales}}{\text{Total assets}} \quad = \quad \text{lower}$$

The turnover of cash ratio is lower, which means you don't need so much liquidity to support the amount of sales. In other words, you have cash that isn't properly working for you.

$$\frac{\text{Net sales}}{\text{Working capital}} \quad = \quad \text{lower}$$

The inventory turnover ratio is also lower, which indicates too much inventory to support the lower sales amount.

$$\frac{\text{Net sales}}{\text{Average inventory}} \quad = \quad \text{lower}$$

Below is a diagram of how the ratios are related. This network of interrelationships illustrates which ratios are affected directly and indirectly when either the numerator or denominator is changed. The ratios connected by a solid line are the ones directly affected. The ratios connected by a dashed line are the ones indirectly affected.

Network of Ratio Interrelationships

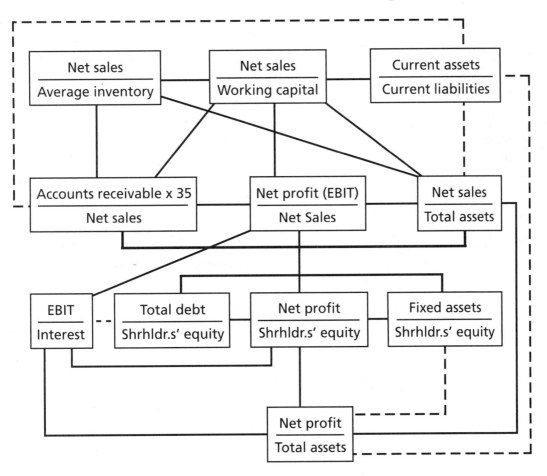

The Makeup of Ratios

Another way of looking at the interaction of ratios is to look behind them for their makeup. For instance, the return on investment ratio is made up of net profit and shareholders' equity. Net profit is found on the income statement as net earnings. Shareholders' equity is found on the balance sheet.

Net earnings is the result of subtracting the cost of goods sold, the operating expenses, and the interest charges and taxes from the net sales. All of these four costs or expenses are made up of individual items that could be reduced to increase the net earnings. Also, sales could be increased. The reduction method may cause a problem in the long run—especially if expenses are cut by not paying bills, or by buying lower quality, less expensive goods to lower the cost of goods sold. If sales are increased by loose credit terms, this could come back to haunt you a few months later when accounts receivable greatly increase. And remember, increasing net earnings doesn't necessarily mean an inflow of cash.

Shareholders' equity (capital stock + paid-in capital + retained earnings) is the result of subtracting liabilities from assets. Shareholders' equity could be reduced by increasing liabilities, or reducing retained earnings, or decreasing assets. (Remember the changes in financial position statement in Part 2.) This may require some explanation at the annual meeting, but it's the way the numbers work.

There are several ways of achieving a different ratio. The smart manager will study the effects of the various actions to determine the best method.

Checklist

I'll remember…

- ❏ to check all relationships between ratios when I make a change for planning purposes, and when a ratio is changed through the natural order of business.

- ❏ that there are five ratios that have net sales as the numerator or denominator.

- ❏ that a ratio may be changed three ways: change the numerator, the denominator, or change both.

- ❏ that a good change in one ratio may be bad for the overall business.

- ❏ that a balance is necessary to have a healthy business.

- ❏ to check the ratio relationship diagram when I am thinking about a change.

- ❏ that most ratios are made up of many accounting transactions from the balance sheet or the income statement.

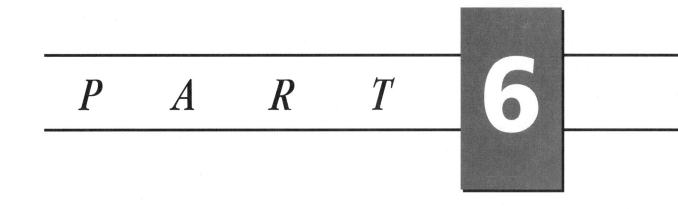

P   A   R   T   6

Financial

Planning

Financial Planning

Effective decisions are crucial to every manager. They lead to promotions and job status. They require the ability to make forecasts and think ahead. Forecasts are sometimes called "what if" exercises.

Anything involving the use of company funds normally requires strong justification. If borrowing is contemplated, this means spending time with finance staff and/or a banker. You'll need to prepare detailed financial information, such as the discounted rate of return and the cost of capital. You will also need to spend time with your marketing department to perform sales research, and with the engineers to check building costs. All this takes time and money.

This part of the book presents three quick decision-shaping tools. These tools will help you to establish if you are in the ballpark, whether there is a chance of an appropriate payback, and if the project is worth spending the time and effort to prepare a detailed proposal for top management.

The three planning tools are:

1 **Break-even analysis** (for product planning)

2 **Decision-tree analysis** (for building or equipment)

3 **Cost-benefit analysis** (for capital purchases)

Break-Even Analysis

Break-even analysis is a good, inexpensive screening technique. It can help you determine whether or not it's worthwhile to do a more intensive and costly analysis.

Break-even analysis provides a handle for designing product specifications. For example, each design has implications for costs. Costs obviously affect price and marketing feasibility. Break-even analysis lets you compare the costs and prices of various designs before the specifications are decided. Using break-even analysis, you can first test the feasibility of a new product on paper, rather than actually going into production and testing the market.

Break-even analysis can be a substitute for estimating an unknown factor in making project decisions. If most expenses are known, the other two variables, profit and demand, may be varied. The analysis can help determine the cash flow, the level of demand needed, and what combination of price and demand will yield the desired profit.

For instance, suppose a manager at JOG Corporation has an idea for a new product. He or she wants to get a quick feel of its feasibility and break-even point. The following examples will provide two means for doing this—with a formula and with a graph.

Break-Even Formula

The formula is:

$$\text{Break-even sales} = \text{fixed costs} + \text{variable costs}$$
$$\text{Be} = F + V$$

Example 1: Suppose the fixed costs are \$100,000, and the variable costs are 66.7% of the break-even sales.

$$\text{Be} = \$100,000 + 66.7\%\text{Be}$$

By simple algebra,

$$\text{Be} - 66.7\%\text{Be} = \$100,000$$

$$33.3\%\text{Be} = \$100,000$$

$$\text{Be} = \frac{\$100,000}{33.3\%}$$

$$\text{Be} = \$300,000 \text{ (by rounding)}$$

Example 2: Now suppose the fixed costs have doubled to \$200,000, and the variable costs are 55% of the break-even sales.

$$\text{Be} = \$200,000 + 55\%\text{Be}$$

By simple algebra,

$$\text{Be} - 55\%\text{Be} = \$200,000$$

$$45\%\text{Be} = \$200,000$$

$$\text{Be} = \frac{\$200,000}{45\%}$$

$$\text{Be} = \$445,000 \text{ (by rounding)}$$

Break-Even Graphs

Let's look again at the first example. The fixed costs are $100,000 and the variable costs are 66.7% of the break-even sales. Suppose the selling price of the product is $7.50 per unit. The following graph plots (a) sales revenue and (b) production cost against the number of units produced. Where the two lines cross is the break-even point.

Break-Even Graph 1

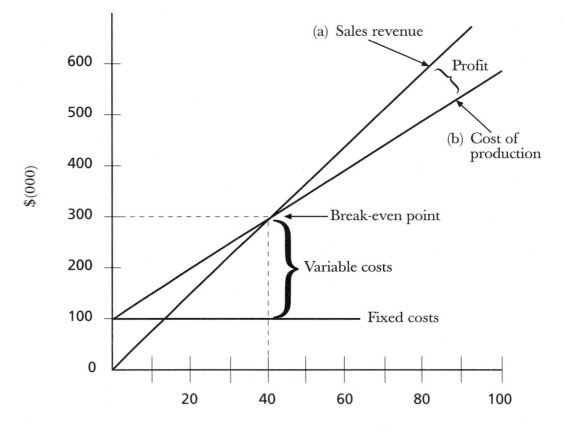

Thousands of Units Produced

If the fixed costs are $200,000 and the variable costs are 55% of the break-even sales, we have the following graph.

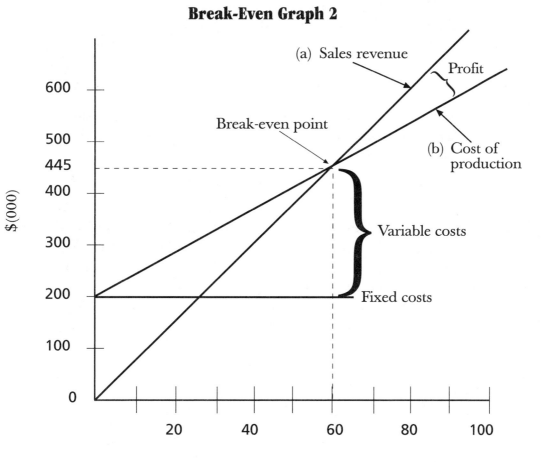

Break-Even Graph 2

(a) Sales revenue

Profit

Break-even point

(b) Cost of production

Variable costs

Fixed costs

$(000)

Thousands of Units Produced

Margin of Safety

Break-even analysis can also help determine a margin of safety. The *margin of safety* is the excess of actual, or budgeted, sales over break-even sales. It can be expressed as dollars or production units.

To calculate the margin of safety, subtract the break-even sales revenue from the total sales revenue and divide by the total sales revenue. For instance, suppose the sales of the new product are 275,000 units. The product sells at $7.50, so the total sales revenue is $7.50 x 275,000 = $2,062,500.

Example 1: The fixed expenses are $100,000. As we previously calculated, the break-even sales revenues is approximately $300,000.

$$\$2,062,500 - \$300,000 \quad = \quad \frac{\$1,762,500}{\$2,062,500} \quad = \quad 85\% \text{ safety margin}$$

Example 2: The fixed expenses are $200,000, and the break-even sales revenue is approximately $445,000.

$$\$2,062,500 - \$445,000 \quad = \quad \frac{\$1,617,500}{\$2,062,500} \quad = \quad 78\% \text{ safety margin}$$

The higher fixed expenses resulted in a lower margin of safety, because the break-even point required more sales. This shows that the principle of leverage (discussed in the next section) works two ways. During good sales times it provides more profit; during slow sales times, the fixed expenses can be a burden.

Leverage

Break-even analysis helps with leverage calculations which relate changes in sales to changes in income. There are two types of leverage: operating and financial. Operating leverage comes from fixed expenses, such as maintenance, rent, and some utilities. Financial leverage results from interest payments on debt incurred by borrowing or by issuing bonds.

Operating Leverage

Operating leverage results when fluctuations in revenue produce wider fluctuations in operating income. That is, once the break-even point is reached, a small change in sales will result in a larger change in operating income. This is because once the fixed charges are covered, only the variable costs (those that are a result of volume, such as raw materials) remain to be covered, so the operating income increases faster.

The formula is:

$$\frac{\text{Revenue} - \text{Variable costs}}{\text{Revenue} - \text{Variable costs} - \text{Fixed costs}} = \frac{\text{Marginal contribution}}{\text{Operating income}}$$

Example 1: Suppose the projected sales are $1,500,000; the break-even point is $300,000; the fixed expenses are about $100,000 or 33.3%, and the variable expenses are about 66.6% of the projected sales revenue.

$$\frac{\$1,500,000 - \$1,000,000}{\$1,500,000 - \$1,000,000 - \$100,000} = \frac{\$500,000}{\$400,000} = 1.25 \text{ times}$$

This example could be tabulated as follows:

Units Sold	Sales ($)	Operating Expenses	Operating Profit (EBIT) ($)
0	0	100,000	(100,000)
40,000	300,000	300,000	0
100,000	750,000	600,000	150,000
200,000	1,500,000	1,100,000	400,000
300,000	2,250,000	1,600,000	650,000

Leverage (CONTINUED)

Example 2: The projected sales are $1,500,000; the break-even point is $445,000; the fixed expenses are about $200,000 or 45% of the break-even revenue; and the variable expenses are about 55% of the projected sales revenue. (Rounding to even numbers is used to keep the calculation simple.)

$$\frac{\$1,500,000 - \$825,000}{\$1,500,000 - \$825,000 - \$200,000} = \frac{\$675,000}{\$475,000} = 1.42 \text{ times}$$

This results in about a 19% increase in operating income from when fixed expenses were doubled on the same amount of sales revenue.

Units Sold	Sales ($)	Operating Expenses	Operating Profit (EBIT) ($)
0	0	200,000	(200,000)
60,000	445,000	445,000	0
100,000	750,000	613,000	137,000
200,000	1,500,000	1,025,000	475,000
300,000	2,250,000	1,438,000	812,000

Leverage varies at each level of production because of the changing weight fixed expenses have to total expenses. Operating leverage decreases as the company's sales increase. Other things being equal, the higher a firm's operating leverage, the higher its risk.

These examples may also be graphed. Break-Even Graph 1, in the previous section, shows a gap between the sales-revenue line and the cost-of-production line for production greater than 40,000 units.

On Break-Even Graph 2, the gap begins after 60,000 units. Break-Even Graph 2 shows more leverage than Graph 1.

Remember, if sales revenue does not materialize to cover the increase in fixed expenses, JOG Corporation will lose faster than if it had a lower break-even point.

Financial Leverage

Financial leverage results from the use of funds in return for a fixed payment, such as an interest payment. The greater the degree that interest expenses are covered, the lower the degree of financial leverage.

The higher the use, the more the leverage and the greater the risk placed on the common shareholders. Financial leverage is determined by:

$$\frac{\text{Revenue} - \text{Variable cost} - \text{Fixed cost}}{\text{Revenue} - \text{Variable cost} - \text{Fixed cost} - \text{Interest}} = \frac{\text{Operating income}}{\text{Earnings before taxes}}$$

JOG Corporation's income statement showed interest payments of $278,000. Let's use this number in connection with the two different operating leverage ratios we just worked and see if it makes a difference.

Example 1:

$$\frac{\$1,500,000 - \$1,000,000 - \$100,000}{\$1,500,000 - \$1,000,000 - 100,000 - \$278,000} = \frac{\$400,000}{\$122,000} = 3.28 \text{ times}$$

Example 2:

$$\frac{\$1,500,000 - \$825,000 - \$200,000}{\$1,500,000 - \$825,000 - \$200,000 - \$278,000} = \frac{\$475,000}{\$197,000} = 2.41 \text{ times}$$

In the first example the increase was from 1.25 times to 3.28 times. In the second example, the increase was from 1.42 times to 2.41 times. The difference in the increase in financial leverage from operating leverage is the greater coverage of the fixed costs in Example 1.

Now let's combine these two formulas and see what occurs when we have two types of leverage working for us—or against us, as during periods of low sales.

The combined formula is:

$$\frac{\text{Revenue} - \text{Variable cost}}{\text{Revenue} - \text{Variable cost} - \text{Fixed cost}} \times \frac{\text{Revenue} - \text{Variable cost} - \text{Fixed cost}}{\text{Revenue} - \text{Variable cost} - \text{Fixed cost} - \text{Interest}} =$$

$$\frac{\text{Revenue} - \text{Variable cost}}{\text{Revenue} - \text{Variable cost} - \text{Fixed cost} - \text{Interest}} = \frac{\text{Marginal contribution}}{\text{Earnings before taxes}}$$

Substituting the figures from the first example:

$$\frac{\$1,500,000 - \$1,000,000}{\$1,500,000 - \$1,000,000 - \$100,000 - \$278,000} = \frac{\$500,000}{\$122,000} = 4.1 \text{ times}$$

And the second example:

$$\frac{\$1,500,000 - \$825,000}{\$1,500,000 - \$825,000 - \$200,000 - \$278,000} = \frac{\$675,000}{\$197,000} = 3.4 \text{ times}$$

Drawbacks to Using Break-Even Analysis

Break-even analysis does not permit proper examination of cash flow. One appropriate way to make investment or capital-purchasing decisions is to consider the proposed project's cash flow. If the discounted value of the cash flow exceeds the required cash outlay then the project is acceptable, other things being equal.

The use of break-even analysis requires that many restrictive assumptions about cost-revenue relationships be made. It is basically a negative technique, defining constraints rather than looking at benefits.

Break-even analysis is static. It is good for a single point in time, not a period of time.

There are alternative uses for money in any business. This technique considers only one at a time and it does not compare them. It also does not take into consideration economies of scale.

The break-even analysis technique is quite simplistic. It is good for getting a feel and for determining if further study is feasible. But it should not be used for final decisions.

Leverage means risk, and risk under a period of high sales is heavily rewarded. But with low sales it becomes a heavy burden to pay for fixed costs with little sales revenue.

Decision-Tree Analysis

Decision-tree analysis can be a useful tool for the decision maker. By combining decision points with probabilities and costs, better information is available. It should be possible in most decisions to look at a variety of alternatives.

For example, you may want to build a modular plant for later expansion, or increment your new plant construction to take advantage of later information. Or you may want to examine the payoff of building a large plant now. This is what decision-tree analysis helps you to do. It permits each decision point to have more than one choice. If these decision points are charted, they appear as branches—hence the name "decision tree." (See the diagram at the end of this section.)

The following example illustrates some of the uses of decision-tree analysis.

Example of Decision-Tree Analysis

You want to determine whether to build a large or small building.

First, gather information concerning the cost of each size building. A large building would cost $6 million and a small one $4 million. The expected income from the large building is $12 million if there is a high demand, and $7 million if the demand is low. The income from the small building would be $8 million for a high demand and $7 million for a low demand.

Next, arrange the information in a matrix as shown below. (M = millions.)

	Large Building			Small Building		
	Income	**Cost**	**Return**	**Income**	**Cost**	**Return**
High demand	$12M	– $6M	= $6M	$8M	– $4M	= $4M
Low demand	$7M	– $6M	= $1M	$7M	– $4M	= $3M

Now you need to determine whether there will be a high or low demand. This may be done through your own experience, the opinions of various trade associations, your marketing group, universities, suppliers, customers, competitors, trade magazines, or business magazines and newspapers.

From this information, probabilities are assigned as to whether there will be a high or low demand and how strongly you believe it. Let's assume the probability of a high demand would be 60% or .6, and the probability of a low demand would be 40% or .4.

The following matrix shows the expected profits. (M = millions.)

	High Demand		Low Demand		
	Probability	Return	Probability	Return	Payoff
Large building	.6 x	$6M +	.4 x	$1M =	$4M
Small building	.6 x	$4M +	.4 x	$3M =	$3.6M

In this instance, building the large building would be more profitable than building the small building by a difference of $4M – $3.6M = $400,000. With this information a better decision can be made.

The probabilities reflect uncertainty of decision making. By using various probabilities you can usually arrive at a ballpark figure that makes sense to you.

As an exercise, let's go back and see what the difference is if the probabilities are reversed: .4 for a high demand and .6 for a low demand. Calculate the payoff for each type of building, and write the figures in the matrix below.

	High Demand		Low Demand		
	Probability	Return	Probability	Return	Payoff
Large building	.4 x	$6M +	.6 x	$1M =	
Small building	.4 x	$4M +	.6 x	$3M =	

How would this affect your decision?

_____

_____

Now let's consider that you may have more than one decision point. For instance, you might be able to build a small building that can be expanded at a later date if demand increases. This time there is an additional decision point for the small building. You will have three payoffs to compare instead of two: the total payoff for the large building, the total payoff for the small building, and the total payoff for a small building that can be expanded.

We have previously determined the payoff for a large building and a small building with no expansion capabilities, based on a 60% probability of high demand and a 40% probability of low demand. We calculated that for a large building the payoff is $4 million and for a small building the payoff is $3.6 million.

Assume that the cost of expanding the small building is $3 million. High demand would give an income of $12 million, from which we subtract the $4 million initial building cost and the $3 million expansion cost, for a payoff of $5 million. We have to multiply this figure by 60%, as we believe there is only a 60% chance of a high demand. This gives us a high-demand payoff of $3 million for the expanded small building. If there is a low demand, an expansion would not be warranted. In this case, the income would be $7 million minus the $4 million building cost, for a payoff of $3 million. This times 40% gives a low-demand payoff of $1.2 million.

To find the total payoff from a small building with expansion capabilities, we add the high-demand payoff to the low-demand payoff. $3 million plus $1.2 million gives a total payoff of $4.2 million. Compare this to the large-building payoff of $4 million and the small-building payoff of $3.6 million. The logical choice is to build a small building with later expansion capabilities.

Decision-Tree Diagram

Start from the bottom and work upward to the payoffs.

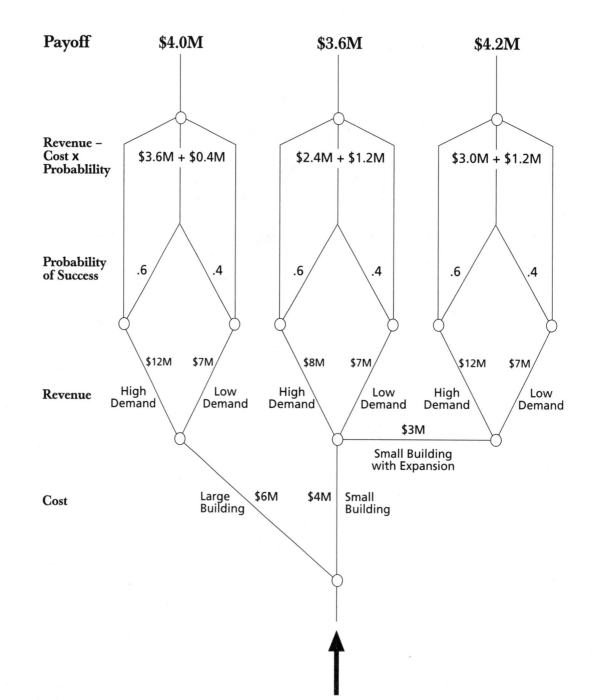

| Payoff | **$4.0M** | **$3.6M** | **$4.2M** |

Revenue –
Cost x
Probablility

$3.6M + $0.4M $2.4M + $1.2M $3.0M + $1.2M

Probability
of Success

.6   .4   .6   .4   .6   .4

Revenue

$12M $7M $8M $7M $12M $7M

High   Low   High   Low   High   Low
Demand Demand Demand Demand Demand Demand

$3M

Small Building
with Expansion

Cost

Large $6M $4M   Small
Building   Building

Cost-Benefit Analysis

The term "capital budgeting" essentially means matching the available funds with the most beneficial use of those funds. This should provide a common basis for evaluating investment opportunities and projects for the company.

Capital budgeting also means that the benefit is for the long term—more than one year. This applies to buildings and equipment as well as research and public relations enhancement. A quick way to compare two different proposals or projects, especially if they are for tangible items, is a cost-benefit analysis. This measures the relationship between anticipated returns and costs. The cost-benefit analysis measures the anticipated return on investment.

The example below compares the costs and benefits of purchasing new equipment. Assume that the new equipment will raise the production cost from $.90 to $1.00 per unit.

	Current Equipment	New Equipment
Units produced annually	100,000	125,000
Sales value at $1.50 per unit	$ 150,000	$ 187,500
Direct cost of the units produced	90,000	125,000
Gross profit	$ 60,000	$ 62,500
Annual benefit		$ 2,500

Assuming constant sales, the total benefit is the annual benefit of $2,500 multiplied by the useful life of the new equipment. These quick calculations should be discounted by the expected inflation rate to get a discounted rate of return over the years of useful life or expected income.

The figures can be adjusted for probability of success, taking the discounted income times the probability of success. For instance, if the new equipment has a useful life of five years and the income is discounted by 10%, the costs and benefits of purchasing it will be as shown in the following table.

Year	FAIRLY CERTAIN			MODERATE			RISKY		
	Income	Probability of Success	New	Income	Probability of Success	New	Income	Probability of Success	New
1	$2,500	1.0	$2,500	$2,500	1.0	$2,500	$2,500	.9	$2,250
2	2,065	1.0	2,065	2,065	.9	1,859	2,065	.8	1,652
3	1,878	1.0	1,878	1,878	.8	1,502	1,878	.7	1,315
4	1,708	1.0	1,708	1,708	.7	1,196	1,708	.6	1,025
5	1,553	1.0	1,553	1,553	.6	932	1,553	.5	777
	$9,704		$9,704	$9,704		$7,989	$9,704		$7,019

If the cost of the new equipment, installation, disruption, training, etc., minus the salvage value is less than the risk, it probably should be considered for investment and more study.

Review

For each statement below, circle **T** if you think it is true, or **F** if you think it is false.

1. Break-even analysis is an expensive and time-consuming tool. **T**   **F**

2. Break-even analysis can be used for product design, equipment purchase and production analysis. **T**   **F**

3. All financial planning tools have some shortcomings and should not be used for final decisions. **T**   **F**

4. Decision-tree analysis helps to understand the feasibility of constructing different-size buildings. **T**   **F**

5. Cost-benefit analysis does not allow you to take into account the probabilities or the discounted rate of return. **T**   **F**

Answers: 1. F, 2. T, 3. T, 4. T, 5. F

Match each formula to its definition by connecting them with a line.

Formula	Definition
1. $\dfrac{\text{Revenue} - \text{Variable costs}}{\text{Revenue} - \text{Variable costs} - \text{Fixed costs}}$	A. $\dfrac{\text{Operating income}}{\text{Earnings before taxes}}$
2. $\dfrac{\text{Revenue} - \text{Variable costs} - \text{Fixed costs}}{\text{Revenue} - \text{Variable costs} - \text{Fixed costs} - \text{Interest}}$	B. $\dfrac{\text{Marginal contribution}}{\text{Earnings before taxes}}$
3. $\dfrac{\text{Revenue} - \text{Variable costs}}{\text{Revenue} - \text{Variable costs} - \text{Fixed costs} - \text{Interest}}$	C. $\dfrac{\text{Marginal contribution}}{\text{Operating income}}$

Answers: 1. C, 2. A, 3. B

Choose **A**, **B**, or **C** by putting a check mark in the appropriate box.

1. Break-even analysis helps to
   - ❏ A. compute costs and benefits.
   - ❏ B. determine probabilities.
   - ❏ C. understand how many units of a product we must sell before we begin to realize a profit.

2. The two types of leverage are
   - ❏ A. balance sheet and income statement.
   - ❏ B. high and low.
   - ❏ C. operational and financial.

3. Decision-tree analysis helps you to
   - ❏ A. determine payoff for two or more alternatives under various economic conditions.
   - ❏ B. determine what trees to plant at your corporation.
   - ❏ C. determine the break-even point.

4. Decision-tree analysis involves the use of
   - ❏ A. cost and revenue.
   - ❏ B. cost, revenue, and demand.
   - ❏ C. cost, revenue, and probable demand.

5. Cost-benefit analysis measures
   - ❏ A. the cost of a project.
   - ❏ B. the anticipated returns and costs.
   - ❏ C. the returns of any project.

6. Cost-benefit analysis
   - ❏ A. can make use of probabilities.
   - ❏ B. can be used to measure your popularity.
   - ❏ C. is the discounted rate of return.

Answers: 1. C, 2. C, 3. A, 4. C, 5. B, 6. A

Reading an Annual Report

How to Read an Annual Report

The annual report to the shareholders generally looks to the past, and it is in management's best interest to present the corporation in a good light. Therefore expect to read a lot of positive words. Also, some auditors seem not to be as independent as they pretend. They tend to use terms like "generally accepted accounting principles," of which there are many. And they usually don't certify that the financial condition reflects a true picture. The phrasing goes something like, "the financial statements present fairly the financial position of...."

However, annual reports do have their place, and if properly used they can supply a lot of valuable information. Annual reports are important for:

➤ Managers within the corporation

➤ Creditors

➤ Potential and current investors

➤ Potential and current vendors and suppliers

Corporate managers usually have their own detailed statements. Their particular area may be only one line on a consolidated statement in the annual report, but their area figures are a part of the consolidated statement.

Potential investors, creditors, and vendors will certainly want to know the debt situation and how fast the corporation pays its bills and collects its receivables. In addition, all users will want to review the yearly 10-K statement, the prospectus which is issued when the corporation sells new securities, and the 10-Q statement, which is like the 10-K statement only it is issued quarterly and is usually more current. They should also keep up with stories and articles concerning their industry and any analysis a broker may supply. The Internet is becoming an important tool for locating valuable corporate information quickly.

Note: 10-K and 10-Q are issued for public companies only.

Start at the Back

An annual report is usually divided into these general categories:

➤ The CEO's letter

➤ Financial statements (balance sheet, income statement, cash-flow statement, and statement of shareholders' equity)

➤ Footnotes

➤ Explanations, analysis, and/or strengths

➤ Report by independent auditors

The report by independent auditors is usually at the back of an annual report. This is the place to start your analysis.

If there is more than the standard two-paragraph statement about auditing and "appropriate tests" and "consistent with generally accepted accounting principles," watch out. Words like "subject to" and "as reported by" may mean the report is okay only if you can believe what the company says about a situation. If the auditor emphasizes things that are also in other places in the report, be suspicious that something may not be quite right. The audit statement should be short and unqualified.

Footnotes

Next, go to the footnotes and look to see if the corporation has changed accounting principles or methods. When a corporation changes its accounting method, it may be trying to make the figures look better. For instance, has the depreciation period been extended? Is it because the assets haven't been working as hard as they first thought and now they will have a longer life? It could be that sales haven't grown as projected. Sometimes the whole story is told in the footnotes. There must be sufficient footnotes to clearly explain, but not enough to obfuscate.

Another reason to change accounting methods is that earnings are up because of a windfall that won't happen again and management wants to store part of it for when sales are down or to stretch out tax payments. Or are earnings down because of a change in accounting, not sales? This, by the way, may be good.

Following are some of the items that appear in the footnotes, with explanations of what they really mean.

Big hit: Taking the last three years' losses in one quarter. This is usually done by a new CEO so he can blame the losses on past management by saying only he had the courage to purify the company. You are supposed to believe things will really get better now. (Maybe they will.)

Depreciation and inventory: The many transactions that can be done with these two have been covered elsewhere in this book. New ones are being discovered everyday. However, the tax rules also change—and they play a large part in the way corporations do business.

Equalizing: Concealing a lucky big gain. The CEO knows such a gain won't happen again, and he doesn't want to have to live up to it in the next two or three quarters. So the financial office comes up with a special account called "reserve for a rainy day" or something or other. The extra income is put away so that it can be called upon the next time earnings are low.

Expense deferral: Spreading the cost of getting customers over their lifetime. Well, maybe over two or three years. This can cause a jump in profits because expenses are not all taken in the year they occurred.

Taking a percentage of completion: Management has decided to take the profit and charge the expenses of a long-term contract, as they believe they are making progress. This may be done even when no money has been received. It helps to spread the wealth more evenly over time, especially for tax purposes.

Financial Statements

Next move to the balance sheet and income statement and compare the ratios of all the years presented. Pay particular attention to receivables and inventory. If the report doesn't furnish the ratios, you ought to do them yourself. Ask questions like: Are receivables and inventories growing faster than sales? Does this mean the company is trying to increase or maintain sales through a lax credit policy? Is the company keeping the plant operating at a higher level without sales, or is this an inventory buildup prior to the big sales season? Check the current ratio and see if the company is paying on time and has an aggressive receivables collection policy.

Another area to watch is long-term debt. It may be expanding; if the company is growing this is usually good. However, if sales are leveling out it may not be so good.

Check asset values by comparing them to those of similar companies. Are they overestimated? Is there an explanation? Remember that overestimated asset values, even with logical reasons, are really not too meaningful without eager buyers.

Look for differences. This means comparing one year with another and the current annual report with past reports. Look for cash flow over time and what is done with it. Is the money reinvested, paid out in dividends, or used paying off heavy debt? Remember, a lot depends on the industry, the age of the company, and the business cycle.

Check the net sales figure. Are sales increasing, remaining steady, or dropping off? If the sales figures are dropping off, this may signal trouble. Sales should keep up with inflation. But they may be down for legitimate reasons—for example, if part of the company was sold. That part may have been unprofitable, and even with lower sales, profits may be up.

Some people go immediately to earnings per share (EPS). But this figure can be misleading, if part of the corporation has been sold, or if there has been a decrease in advertising or research and development, or if there has been a postponement of some expenses that cause the earnings to rise. Also, earnings per share will vary under different accounting methods. They do not reflect risk to the company or a division of the company. Earnings per share do not account for the investment required for working capital or fixed capital needs. So if these needs or expenses are shorted to make the earnings look good in the short term, be careful about the long term.

CEO's Letter

The fourth place to look is the president's or CEO's letter. This will provide clues about the workings of the corporation. It should be in tune with what you have already found out. In the letter, watch for weak words such as "we're working on it," "continuing toward," "nearly complete," "considered to be," and "except for." Also watch for words that sound like an apology, or that are more modifiers than action words when the writer analyzes changes in sales, debt, or profit.

The letter should explain in easily understood language what has happened, where the company is going, how it will get there, and why. A lot of letters don't. The usual letter is one or two pages long. A good one will tell it like it is, warts and all. This type of letter may run 15 or more pages—but really good letters are rare.

By the way, the financial statements in the annual report are usually not the ones the IRS sees. But differences must be disclosed. Check the footnotes carefully. For example, depreciation may be calculated by the straight-line method for the annual report, but by an accelerated method for the IRS. Also, the inventory is usually reported as average inventory in the annual report, but as last-in-first-out or first-in-first-out in tax returns. This is a way of lowering taxes but it may not be clearly mentioned.

Explanations, Analysis and/or Report by Independent Auditor

Finally, look at the explanations and analysis provided. Note whether stock has been sold and what the proceeds were used for. Was it used to expand the plant to meet improving sales? Or was it used to pay off debt? If possible, see how much stock is held by the company officers and board members. Are they buying or selling? Also check for the qualifications of top management, if available.

Look for legal disputes. Have they been settled? Who are they with—the IRS, creditors, customers, or the EPA? Note how long they have been going on. Almost any company may have a sound reason to disagree with a government agency, but a dispute with a creditor or a customer may signal trouble.

In general, auditors do their jobs right. They do not provide approval or endorsements for the company. They only provide reasonable assurance that the numbers presented do not intentionally distort the company's financial position.

Checklist

❏ I will check the annual report by starting with the auditors' statement.

❏ I will watch for weak words like "subject to," "working on it," "nearly complete," and "except for."

❏ I will compare the past 5-10 years' ratios to obtain a better understanding of what has really happened.

❏ I will look at other reports, such as the 10-K and the prospectus, if new stock has been issued.

❏ I will keep up with business readings and articles on the Internet, especially those affecting my industry.

❏ I will be careful if there are numerous footnotes.

❏ I understand that there may be two financial statements, the one in the annual report and the one for tax purposes submitted to the IRS.

NOTES

NOTES

Now Available From

Books•Videos•CD-ROMs•Computer-Based Training Products

Subject Areas Include:

Management
Human Resources
Communication Skills
Personal Development
Marketing/Sales
Organizational Development
Customer Service/Quality
Computer Skills
Small Business and Entrepreneurship
Adult Literacy and Learning
Life Planning and Retirement

CRISP WORLDWIDE DISTRIBUTION

English language books are distributed worldwide. Major international distributors include:

ASIA/PACIFIC

Australia/New Zealand: In Learning, PO Box 1051, Springwood QLD, Brisbane, Australia 4127   Tel: 61-7-3-841-2286, Facsimile: 61-7-3-841-1580
ATTN: Messrs. Gordon

Philippines: National Book Store Inc., Quad Alpha Centrum Bldg, 125 Pioneer Street, Mandaluyong, Metro Manila, Philippines   Tel: 632-631-8051, Facsimile: 632-631-5016

Singapore, Malaysia, Brunei, Indonesia: Times Book Shops. Direct sales HQ: STP Distributors, Pasir Panjang Distrientre, Block 1 #03-01A, Pasir Panjang Rd, Singapore 118480   Tel: 65-2767626, Facsimile: 65-2767119

Japan: Phoenix Associates Co., Ltd., Mizuho Bldng, 3-F, 2-12-2, Kami Osaki, Shinagawa-Ku, Tokyo 141   Tel: 81-33-443-7231, Facsimile: 81-33-443-7640
ATTN: Mr. Peter Owans

CANADA

Crisp Learning Canada, 60 Briarwood Avenue, Mississauga, ON L5G 3N6 Canada
Tel: (905) 274-5678, Facsimile: (905) 278-2801
ATTN: Mr. Steve Connolly/Mr. Jerry McNabb

Trade Book Stores: Raincoast Books, 8680 Cambie Street,
Vancouver, BC V6P 6M9 Canada
Tel: (604) 323-7100, Facsimile: (604) 323-2600   ATTN: Order Desk

EUROPEAN UNION

England: Flex Training, Ltd., 9-15 Hitchin Street,
Baldock, Hertfordshire, SG7 6A, England
Tel: 44-1-46-289-6000, Facsimile: 44-1-46-289-2417   ATTN: Mr. David Willetts

INDIA

Multi-Media HRD, Pvt., Ltd., National House,
Tulloch Road, Appolo Bunder, Bombay, India 400-039
Tel: 91-22-204-2281, Facsimile: 91-22-283-6478   ATTN: Messrs. Aggarwal

SOUTH AMERICA

Mexico: Grupo Editorial Iberoamerica, Nebraska 199, Col. Napoles, 03810 Mexico, D.F.
Tel: 525-523-0994, Facsimile: 525-543-1173   ATTN: Señor Nicholas Grepe

SOUTH AFRICA

Alternative Books, PO Box 1345, Ferndale 2160, South Africa
Tel: 27-11-792-7730, Facsimile: 27-11-792-7787   ATTN: Mr. Vernon de Haas